诸子百家智慧故事

Wisdom of Ancient Chinese Sages

WISDOM of CONFUCIUS

孔子智慧故事

主编 陶黎铭 张 英

中文作者 厉 琳

英文作者 束慧娟

英文审订 汪榕培

Editors-in-Chief *Tao Liming* *Zhang Ying*

Chinese by *Li Lin*

English by *Shu Huijuan*

Revised by *Wang Rongpei*

上海外语教育出版社

外教社 SHANGHAI FOREIGN LANGUAGE EDUCATION PRESS

图书在版编目(CIP)数据

孔子智慧故事 / 历琳著；束慧娟译.
—上海：上海外语教育出版社，2010
(诸子百家智慧故事丛书)
ISBN 978-7-5446-1820-5

I. 孔… II. ①历… ②束… III. 孔丘－哲学思想－通俗读物
—汉、英 IV. B222.2-49

中国版本图书馆CIP数据核字(2010)第075270号

出版发行：上海外语教育出版社
（上海外国语大学内） 邮编：200083
电　　话：021-65425300（总机）
电子邮箱：bookinfo@sflep.com.cn
网　　址：http://www.sflep.com.cn http://www.sflep.com
责任编辑：李　欣

印　　刷：常熟高专印刷有限公司
开　　本：890×1240 1/32 印张 7.25 字数 220 千字
版　　次：2010 年 12 月第 1 版 2010 年 12 月第 1 次印刷
印　　数：5 000 册

书　　号：ISBN 978-7-5446-1820-5 / B・0009
定　　价：30.00 元

前　言

2000多年前的春秋战国时代，是中国各种思想流派百花齐放的时期，涌现了孔子、孟子、老子、庄子、墨子、荀子、孙子、韩非子等思想家、哲学家，他们开创了儒、道、墨、法等各具特色、影响深远的思想派别，后世称为“诸子百家”。“诸子百家智慧故事”是一套介绍先秦诸子经典的汉英对照系列丛书，将先秦诸子的生平事迹、哲学思想、格言警句、哲理寓言以及与他们有关的历史故事串联成启迪智慧的短小故事，既能满足中国读者的普及型阅读需求，又照顾到国外读者的文化特点，让大家在轻松愉快的阅读氛围中走近春秋战国时代“百家争鸣”的先哲们。

为了让世界更好地了解中国的经典文化，“诸子百家智慧故事”在编写上突出了以下三个特点：

轻松阅读——本系列每本书中文不过七八万字，每个故事就是一个相对独立的阅读单位，仅几百字的内容十分钟就能读完，在当今信息爆炸的快节奏时代，这种文本便于读者随时取出翻阅。

经济阅读——中国的文字，特别是古文字，常常是外国人阅读中国经典的障碍，本丛书采取汉英双语对照，中文是浅显易懂的白话体，配以通顺晓畅的英语译文，读者无须钻研艰深的典籍，就能了解先哲的智慧。

趣味阅读——本丛书通过一个个短小生动的故事以及古意盎然的插图，为读者深入浅出地解读诸子经典。

先秦诸子经典是中国的宝贵精神财富，至今在中国乃至全世界都有广泛的影响。希望本丛书能够引起广大中外读者对先秦诸子百家的兴趣，并能通过书中的故事体会到博大精深的中国智慧。

Preface

Over two millennia ago, China experienced a boom of ideas and philosophies in the form of "100 Schools of Thought". Confucius, Mencius, Laozi, Zhuangzi, Mozi, Xunzi, Hanfeizi, Sun Tzu ... These are the stellar names behind the philosophical schools like Confucianism, Taoism, Mohism, Legalism, etc. in the Spring and Autumn Period and the Warring States Period (from 770 BC to 221 BC). The classics of these ancient sages contain great wisdom and have exerted profound influence on Chinese history and thought. While the classics themselves may seem difficult to understand today, you can find lucid and accessible explanations of the ancient philosophies in the books of *Wisdom of Ancient Chinese Sages*. With the help of a collection of short and interesting stories, you can get to know the lives and thoughts of the ancient sages, the axioms and allegories they employed to illustrate their ideas, and some facts about the historical era they lived in.

With the aim of presenting the ancient Chinese classics to the world audience, *Wisdom of Ancient Chinese Sages* boasts three advantages:

Easiness — Each book in the series is comprised of only a few dozen stories, each of which has no more than 2,000 words and can be glanced through in a 10-minute coffee break. Even in your busy life, you can always snatch some time to enjoy a story of wisdom and gain some spiritual nourishment.

Efficiency — The classics may seem a little obscure today since they are written in the ancient Chinese. In this Chinese-English version of *Wisdom of Ancient Chinese Sages*, however, the classics are rendered in simple, everyday English. Without having to tax your brains, you can readily comprehend the profound wisdom of the ancient sages.

Attractiveness — With all the short but lively stories accompanied by beautiful illustrations, *Wisdom of Ancient Chinese Sages* explains to you the ancient philosophical ideas in a friendly and agreeable way.

The ancient philosophical classics in the "100 Schools of Thought" are an important spiritual heritage of China and impose great cultural reverberations beyond the Chinese borders. We hope that the series may let the readers develop an interest in the ancient Chinese sages and their philosophies, and appreciate the quintessential Chinese wisdom that may prove useful in present day.

目录

Contents

孔子生平
The Life of Confucius

孔子（公元前551年—前479年），名丘，字仲尼，鲁国人，是中国春秋（公元前770年—前476年）后期思想家、教育家，儒家的创始人。

孔子的祖先可以追溯到商朝。但我们一般说他是宋国贵族的后代，他的先祖为了躲避宋国内乱而移居到鲁国。公元前1046年，周武王讨伐商纣王，灭掉了商朝。周王朝分封了众多的诸侯国：黄河下游有宋、卫、齐、鲁、陈、蔡、郑等国；黄河中上游有晋、秦、虞、虢等国；长江流域有楚、吴、越等国。其中宋国是当时被灭的纣王的庶兄微子启的封地。微子启的嫡传后代弗父何礼让了国君之位，美名四传。而弗父何的曾孙正考文辅佐了宋国的三朝君主，为人谦恭俭朴，十分熟悉古代文献，当时的人都对他赞不绝口。这弗父何就是孔子的第十代先祖，正考文是孔子的第七代先祖。到了正考文的儿子孔父嘉（孔子的第六代先祖）的时候，宋国发生内乱，贵族内讧，孔父嘉被杀。他的后代因此逃到了鲁国，开始以“孔”作为姓氏。

孔子的父亲名纥，字叔梁。在他之前已有五代生活在鲁国，却都没有什么作为，默默无闻，世袭贵族的特权也早就失去了。但是叔梁纥在鲁国却有些名声。他身强体壮，孔武有力，以英勇无畏的气概立下过两次战功，被任命为陬邑大夫，官职虽然不大，却受到世人的仰慕。叔梁纥虽然有了名声，但他并不满意自己的生活。他的妻子姓施，给他生了九个女儿，却没有儿子；他的小妾倒是给他生了一个儿子，却是跛脚。按照当时严格的礼仪规矩，只有身体健康、相貌端庄的男性后代才能祭祀祖先的神灵，身有残缺就不能承担祭祀祖先的重任。叔梁纥年事已高，却没有个身体健全的儿子，自己百年后岂不是断了祭祀祖宗的人？他很着急，想办法尽快再生个儿子。

孔子的母亲叫颜徵在，嫁给叔梁纥的时候只有16岁。颜徵在的父亲叫颜襄，祖上也是贵族，到了颜襄的时候也已经没落，但他自己还是很有文化修养，也教孩子们知书达理。叔梁纥来颜家求亲，颜家的小女儿便嫁给了他。两人年龄相差很大，而且没有经过订婚三年后再嫁娶的礼节便急急忙忙成亲了，这在当时是很受非议的。到司马迁写《史记·孔子世家》的时候，还把孔子的出生说成是叔梁纥和颜徵在野合的结果——不符合当时的礼仪。这大概是因为叔梁纥年龄太大，想不耽搁时间，尽快有个儿子的缘故。

叔梁纥和颜徵在结婚后很希望生儿子，便到曲阜东南方的尼丘山去祷告神灵。公元前551年，他们的儿子真的出生了，这便是孔子——他们为他取名"丘"，字仲尼，寓意着在尼丘山祷告来的儿子，叔梁纥的第二个儿子。后人因此也称孔子为"孔老二"。孔子的出生使得叔梁纥极为高兴，但只高兴了三年，在孔子三岁的时候，叔梁纥就抛妻弃子过世了。

父亲死后，孔子跟着母亲回到了外祖父家生活。因为没有社会地位，又没有父亲，家境贫困，孔子小时候的生活自然是艰涩的。妈妈在操持活计之余，也严格教育孔子学习技能谋生，演习礼仪，树立志向。孔子还真的特别喜欢用些泥巴捏成或圆或方的小碗小盘之类的东西玩，喜欢模仿祭祀时候的那种场合，把泥巴玩具像祭祀品一样地陈列起来，自己学着行礼。

孔子喜欢这样的游戏，是跟他生活的鲁国文化环境有关系的。周武王灭掉纣王后，把自己的弟弟周公旦封在了鲁。周公旦是一位很有才能的政治家和军事家，也具有丰富的历史文化知识。周王朝的典章制度和礼仪音乐多半是他制订的。他长期在周王朝执政，因此，鲁国是由他的儿子伯禽代为国君。伯禽很严格地按照周礼的规定管理国家，使得周礼所代表的文化在鲁国得到完善的保存和发展，素有礼乐之邦之称。到春秋末年，礼乐仍然保持完好。鲁国根深蒂固的礼乐传统对孔子有深刻的影响。

后来孔子慢慢长大了，为了帮助母亲维持生计，他开始从事各种劳动，养成勤劳俭朴的习惯，经受困难的磨炼。17 岁，孔子又失去了母亲。他不知道父亲安葬在什么地方，便把母亲的棺木停放在一处叫“五父之衢”的地方，以引起来往行人的注意。他想会有人告诉他答案的。果然，一个老妇人过来告诉他，他父亲安葬在防山，在曲阜东面。孔子因此可以把父母亲合葬在一起，遵从了当时的习俗。孔子也从这件事上，确信自己有着光荣的家世，他应该重振家族威名。

他勤奋好学，看书、思考、求教，逐渐成了博学多才的人。当时对全才的人所要求的六种技艺礼、乐、射、御、书、数，也就是礼节、音乐、射箭、赶车、识字、计算他都刻苦练习，把自己锻炼成文武全才的人。但他依旧很谦虚，从不沾沾自喜。他后来对自己的学生们说，因为得不到从政的机会，所以有了学习这些本事的时间。

19 岁，孔子结婚。20 岁，有了儿子孔鲤。

孔子尽管多才多艺，可并没有得到君王的重视。20 多岁的时候，他有幸得到过两次做小官的机会，一次是做“委吏”，管理仓库，他把每笔进出的账目都搞得非常清楚，没有差错。还有一次是做“乘田”，管理牛羊，他把每头牛每只羊都喂养得肥肥壮壮。尽管职位卑微，他却做得很踏实，很尽心。但是，他还是没有得到更高的提拔。

30岁，孔子真正开始了他一生中最伟大的事业——收学生，教授六艺。他还提出“有教无类”的思想，不分穷富贵贱，让愿意学习的人都能得到受教育的机会。他的学生越来越多，影响越来越大。

34岁，孔子有机会去周的都城洛阳，趁机向当时在洛阳担任保管文物工作的老子求教，增添了更多的文物、礼制等方面的知识。

35岁，鲁国的三家最有实力的贵族孟孙氏、叔孙氏、季孙氏因为矛盾而发生内乱，连国君鲁昭公也逃到了齐国。鲁国处于混乱中，孔子没有办法，只好也离开鲁国，到齐国去寻找机会。

孔子在齐国住了几年，却因为和齐国执政大臣晏婴在政治主张上的对立，没能被齐景公任用。37岁返回鲁国，在鲁国的混乱中寂寞地等待从政实施自己主张的机会。等到公元前510年鲁昭公死在齐国，鲁定公继位，孔子没有得到机会，那年他42岁。又等了五年，把持鲁国国政的季平子死了，可继承他的季桓子依然大权在握，而且季桓子的三大家臣如季桓子威胁鲁定公一般地胁迫季桓子，犯上作乱，孔子还是没有机会施展抱负。这么一晃，孔子便50岁了。这些年里，孔子只能用心在治学施教上，开始整理诗、书、礼、乐，招收弟子一天比一天多，声名大振。

公元前501年，孔子51岁。这一年，孔子终于有了真正从政的机会，他被鲁定公任命为中都宰，就像是今天的首都市长。虽然这是孔子第一次正式担任较重要的官职，但他观察了这么多年的社会冷暖，又时时用心思考，这次从政给了他极好地运用他那些深思熟虑已久的策略的机会，短短一年，政绩斐然，以致鲁国西边的一些国家都想来学习孔子的治理方法。孔子从中都宰升为司空，又从司空升为司寇。他在鲁国推行的政策，让鲁国出现一派欣欣向荣的景象，人们尊老爱幼，路不拾遗，社会安定，风气良好。

孔子在齐国的几年，虽然没得到齐景公的任用，但齐国人都感受到了孔子丰富的知识，深厚的学养及远大的抱负。现在眼见得鲁国在孔子的参政下，社会稳定，人民安居乐业，日渐兴盛，这对齐国来说是个危险因素。齐国便想办法要压服鲁国，于是便有了齐鲁两国的夹谷之会。在夹谷之会上孔子以礼取胜，挫败了齐国的阴谋，还收回了被齐国侵占的三座城池。这一胜利进一步提高了孔子的威望。而齐国也更担心鲁国的崛起。

齐国设下阴谋，挑选了 80 名能歌善舞的美女和 30 辆豪华马车（每车 4 匹骏马）送给鲁国。鲁定公和季桓子都沉醉在这些美女的姿色与歌舞中，不理朝政，孔子也被冷落一旁。孔子开始时还怀着希望等待，但直等到冬至祭祀结束，孔子也没得到祭肉，这意味着孔子已被遗忘。看来，鲁定公与季桓子更需要美女的歌舞，而不在意孔子的政治理想。孔子彻底失望，辞去职务，领着弟子离开鲁国，去寻找能够实现理想的地方。这一年是公元前 497 年，孔子 55 岁。

孔子这一走，就是 14 个春秋。他们先到了卫国，然后往南到了卫国和晋国交界地区的匡城，离开匡城后在晋国边境徘徊了许久，终于还是没有入境，又折回卫国。公元前 492 年再次离开卫国，前往宋国。在宋国这个他祖先的封地上，孔子也没能如愿以偿，而是惶惶逃到了郑国，再从郑国到了陈国，在陈国住了三年。又遇吴国进攻陈国，而楚国前来帮助陈国与吴国对垒，面对战乱，孔子不得不带着弟子离开陈国，往南逃到蔡国。路上遇到吴楚交战，他们被乱兵围住，进退不得。带的粮食吃完了，连着七天没有生火做饭，大家都愁苦不堪。而孔子却泰然处之，告诉弟子们，真正有道德有学问的人是能够处于困境而不动摇自己的理想的，就像松柏，只有经过严寒的冬天，世人才能看出经得起酷寒考验的松柏依旧翠绿。后来大家到了楚国，楚昭王本想重用孔子，却被令尹子西劝阻了，孔子的政治理想终究没有找到生长的土壤。

公元前489年，63岁的孔子返回卫国，又在卫国住了五年，直到68岁，他的政治理想依旧难产。晚年的孔子回首十多年栖栖遑遑没有结果的奔走，无限感慨，也深知自己的政治理想在现实社会中找不到出路。他决定回到鲁国。

公元前484年，年近70的孔子回到了鲁国。开始的时候，鲁哀公和季康子都向他请教政治的大道理。但是，孔子的理想的政治与统治者现实的私利的政治毕竟是不同的，孔子自然不能参加实际的政治，然而他依旧关心政治。晚年的他把文化教育事业作为最根本的活动——只要能发生政治影响，也就是从政，而从政并不一定要供职于政府部门，这是孔子十多年奔波观察思考后的转变。

孔子回到鲁国后，除了教学，整理编写了史书《春秋》，还整理了当时流行的诗歌和音乐，古代诗歌总集《诗经》正是靠了他的整理、提倡才广泛流传的，给后代保存了珍贵的文化艺术遗产。

公元前479年，孔子病逝，终年73岁。

南宋哲学家、教育家朱熹曾经做过一首诗，其中有两句是“天不生仲尼，万古长如夜”。当然，这是诗句，带有文学的夸张，但我们可以从诗句中体会出孔子对中国文化的巨大贡献，对中国人的文化心理结构的深刻影响。这样的贡献与影响在中国可以说孔子是第一人。孔子的学说博大精深，虽含有一些传统的保守的思想因素，但其主流在当时是有利于社会进步的。所以在战国时代得到了进一步的发展，成为先秦显学之一。但由于历史的原因，汉以前并未受到统治者的特别关注。汉代以后，建立起中央集权的封建统治，孔子的思想适合统治阶级的需要，所以受到重视。汉武帝采纳董仲舒的对策，“罢黜百家，独尊儒术”，正式确立了孔子及其学说在中国思想界的统治地位。以后，历代统治者进一步采取了神化孔子、提倡儒学的措施，巩固了孔子的至尊地位。孔子的思想对中国封建社会的哲学、文学、艺术、教育、史学等产生了巨大的影响，作为中国传统文化的杰出代表，这种影响波及东亚乃至全世界。但在漫长的封建社会中，统治阶级出于自身的需要，片面发展了孔子思想中的保守方面，束缚了人们的思想。五四运动以后，孔子思想的保守性受到了进步思想家的批判。现在学者们正用越来越客观的思想和态度对孔子及其学说做出尽量符合历史原貌的评价和解读。孔子提出的“以人为本”的仁爱思想，人伦价值观念、道德理念，“以和为贵”的群体观念，世界大同、天人合一、人与人及人与自然的和谐相处等，甚至“乐天知命”的生活态度对现代社会依旧有深远的影响。

Confucius (551–479 BC) was named Qiu at birth, and styled Zhongni. Born in the State of Lu, he was a thinker, educator, and founder of the Confucian School of Thought in the late Spring and Autumn Period (770–476 BC).

The ancestors of Confucius could be traced to the Shang Dynasty. But his ancestors were generally identified as members of the royal State of Song, and his forefather moved to Lu to escape from the turmoil in Song. In 1046 BC, King Wu of the State of Zhou defeated King Zhou of the Shang Dynasty and put an end to Shang. Thereafter, King Wu conferred noble titles on many vassal states, such as: Song, Wei, Qi, Lu, Chen, Cai, and Zheng in the lower Yellow River area; Jin, Qin, Yu, and Guo in the upper Yellow River region; Chu, Wu, and Yue in the Yangtze basin. Among these, the State of Song was the fief of Weizi Qi, a cousin of the perished king Zhou. Weizi Qi had a direct descendant named Fufu He who abdicated his throne and won himself a good reputation. Fufu He's great-grandson Zheng Kaowen assisted three generations of rulers in Song. His modesty and thrift in administrating the state and his profound knowledge of ancient literature won him popular acclaim. Fufu He was the tenth-generation ancestor of Confucius and Zheng Kaowen was the seventh. By the time of Zheng Kaowen's son Kong Fujia (the sixth-generation ancestor to Confucius), the State of Song was afflicted by turmoil and fraction among the nobles. Kong Fujia was killed and his offsprings escaped to the State of Lu, where Kong (Con) was taken as their surname for the clan.

The Kong clan had long lost their hereditary noble powers

and lived in oblivion for five generations in the State of Lu until Confucius' father Shuliang He who gained some reputation as a warrior for his physical strength and courage. For his feats in two battles with extraordinary valor, Shuliang He was made a *Dafu* in the city of Zou. Though a petty official, he was widely respected. Despite his fame, Shuliang He felt unhappy for his life. His wife Lady Shi bore him 9 daughters without a son while his concubine bore him a crippled boy. The rigid protocol then required a male of regular features and physical soundness to carry on the grand mission of paying sacrifices to the ancestors. As he was getting on in years, he was eager to have a physically sound son to carry forward the family line.

Confucius' mother Yan Zhengzai was married to Shuliang He at the age of 16. Her father Yan Xiang was also a descendent on a declining noble line. Though impoverished, he was quite cultivated and taught his children classics and proprieties. He accepted Shuliang He's proposal and married off his youngest daughter. Despite the big gap in their ages and the conventional three years' waiting after engagement, Shuliang He married his new wife in a haste, which caused quite a bit of criticism from the society. According to the section of "The Family Line of Confucius" in Sima Qian's *Records of the Historian*, Confucius was born from the illicit relationship between Shuliang He and Yan Zhengzai. Obviously it was because Shuliang He could not risk waiting to have a son.

Being too impatient to have a son, Shuliang He and Yan Zhengzai went to Mount Niqiu southeast to Qufu to pray for god's blessing. As luck would have it, they had a son in 551 BC, who was Confucius. They named him Qiu and styled

Zhongni, indicating their praying on Mount Niqiu. Confucius was his second son and hence his nickname was Kong Lao'er (the Kong's second son). Shuliang He was overjoyed by the birth of his second son but his joy was short lived, for he passed away three years later.

Thereupon, the baby Confucius moved back to his grandfather's with his mother. Being fatherless and impoverished, Confucius led a very hard life in his childhood. Besides making a living, his mother attached great importance to Confucius' studies of skills and rites and setting up ambitions. Confucius was fond of making round or square bowls or plates with mud to imitate sacrificial settings, and practicing rites with his mud offerings.

His love for such games had a lot to do with the cultural environments in the State of Lu where he lived. After getting rid of King Zhou of Shang, King Wu of Zhou conferred Lu to his younger brother Duke Dan (Zhougong Dan), who, with his talents in political and military affairs and knowledge of history and culture, stipulated most of the codes, rites and music for the Zhou Dynasty. Zhougong Dan spent most of his time in the Zhou court, leaving the administration of Lu to his son Boqin, who strictly conformed to the Zhou rites in administrating his state, thus contributing to the preservation and development of the Zhou rites in Lu and winning Lu a good fame for practicing rites and music. Toward the end of the Spring and Autumn Period, the rites and music were still well preserved in Lu, and the deep-rooted tradition cast a strong influence on Confucius.

As he grew up, Confucius took up various work to help his mother with their sustenance. He nurtured the diligent and frugal habits when he experienced the vicissitudes of hard life. At the age of 17, Confucius lost his mother. Not knowing where his father was buried, Confucius stationed his mother's coffin on a street by the name of Wu-Fu-Zhi-Qu to invite public attention so that he might find out his father's tomb. It so happened that an old lady came up to tell him that his father's tomb was in Mount Fang to the east of Qufu. Therefore, Confucius could lay both his parents in the same tomb after the custom of his time. That, too, made Confucius believe that he had a shining family history and should revive its reputation.

Diligent and studious, Confucius read and consulted extensively and gradually became erudite and versatile. The canonical standards for an all-rounder in his time included competence on the six classical arts of rites, music, archery, riding, writing, and arithmetic. Confucius trained himself assiduously to be adept with both the pen and the sword. Humble-minded as he was, Confucius never felt complacent for his achievements. Later he explained to his disciples that he had the time to reach his attainments because he could not enter politics.

Confucius got married at the age of 19 and had his son Kong Li in the following year.

For all his versatile talents, Confucius did not receive due attention from the throne. In his twenties, he had the luck to be offered two petty positions — one was a "warehouse keeper" and he reconciled the balance sheets clearly without any errors; the other was a "cattle keeper" and he kept his sheep and cows well fed. He exerted his full efforts in his low positions, but received no further promotion.

At the age of 30, Confucius began the greatest career in his life — recruiting disciples and instructing them the six classical arts. In his teaching he championed the principle of "education for everyone regardless of their social or financial backgrounds". As a result, his disciples increased and his influence expanded.

At the age of 34, Confucius had an opportunity to visit Luoyang, the capital city of the State of Zhou, where he consulted Laozi who was working to preserve cultural relics. Confucius thereby learned more of cultural relics and rites.

At the age of 35, the State of Lu fell into chaos because of the conflicts among the three domineering aristocratic clans — Meng Sun, Shu Sun, and Ji Sun. Even Duke Zhao of Lu had to flee to the State of Qi, leaving his home state in turmoil. Confucius had but to move out of Lu and seek opportunities in Qi.

During the few years of his stay in Qi, Confucius could not find a career from Duke Jing because his political doctrines were in conflict with Minister Yan Ying. At the age of 37, Confucius moved back to Lu, waiting lonely in the turmoil for his time to carry out his political ideals. When Duke Zhao died in 510 BC, Duke Ding succeeded his throne. Confucius was already 42 years old, holding vain hopes. Five more years passed before Ji Ping who dominated the politics died, leaving his power to the hands of Ji Huan. The three retainers menaced Ji Huan just as Ji Huan menaced Duke Ding, keeping the politics in a continued turmoil. Again, Confucius could not give play to his talents. In the blink of an eye, Confucius turned 50. He did his utmost to focus on education and the editing of poetry, calligraphy, rites and music. With his disciples increasing, Confucius rose to even greater fame.

At the age of 51 (501 BC) Confucius had a real opportunity for an official career when he was commissioned as Officer-in-Charge of Zhongdu, an equivalent of today's mayor of the capital city. Though it was his first public office, he eventually had a chance to put his deliberate strategies to full play from his long observation and reflection of the society. Within a matter of one year under his governance, he had made such brilliant accomplishments that his city became a model for neighboring states. He was then elevated to be Director of Engineering and later Minister of Justice. The State of Lu thrived as a result of his policies. People respected the aged and took good care of the young, and no one would pick up lost articles on the road. The society was in peace and stability with fair ethos.

During his years of stay in the State of Qi, Confucius didn't avail himself of patronage from Duke Jing. Nevertheless, his rich knowledge and cultivation as well as his high aspirations became well known among the people of Qi. With Confucius' participation, the State of Lu maintained social stability, with its people living in prosperity and contentment. The thriving Lu, however, was becoming a threat to the neighboring Qi. Therefore, Qi had to find ways to overbear Lu, which turned out to be the historic Jiagu Summit of the two states. Confucius defeated Qi's conspiracy at the summit with his civil and courteous tactics. Moreover, Lu regained the lands of three cities that had been seized by Qi. The victory further enhanced Confucius' prestige, and added to the worries of Qi over the rise of Lu.

Then Qi devised an intrigue to present Lu with 80 beauties who were good at singing and dancing together with 30 luxurious carriages (each driven by four superb horses). Both Duke Ding and Ji Huan indulged themselves in the beauties, neglecting state affairs and Confucius as well. At the start, Confucius cherished some hope until the end of winter solstice when he did not receive the sacrificial meat. He was completely left in oblivion. Duke Ding and Ji Huan were addicted more to the beauties' singing and dancing than to his political ideals. Thoroughly despaired, he quitted his job and led his disciples out of Lu to search for a place where he could realize his ideals. It was the year of 497 BC when Confucius was 55.

After their self-exile, Confucius and his disciples spent 14 years away from the State of Lu. They first reached the State of Wei and proceeded to Kuangcheng city at the border between Wei and Jin. After wandering quite some time along the border of Jin, they retraced their steps to Wei until the year 492 BC when they proceeded to Song. Though he was now in the former fief of his ancestors, Confucius did not attain his end but fled in panic to Zheng and then to Chen, where they stayed for three years. However, the State of Chen was under attack from Wu, and Chu came to Chen's rescue. In face of the battles and chaos, Confucius led his disciples out of Chen to seek shelter in the State of Cai. When they were surrounded halfway by the soldiers of Wu and Chu, they had no way either to advance or retreat. They soon ran out of provisions, and had nothing to cook for seven consecutive days. Everyone was drowned in distress except for Confucius who remained unruffled. He instructed his disciples that one with true virtues and knowledge would not have his ideals stirred in plights, which was comparable to the pines and cypresses that had come through the harsh winter but maintained their viridity. By the time when they made to Chu, King Zhao had intended to put Confucius to an important position, but was dissuaded by Minister Zixi. The roots of Confucius' political ideals still found no soil to grow.

In 489 BC, the 63-year-old Confucius returned to Wei and lived there for five years until he was 68 but could find no way yet to realize his political ideals. Deeply engrossed in the sad recollections of his decade-odd futile years on the go, Confucius came to realize the impossibility of realizing his political ideals and decided to return to Lu.

Confucius returned to Lu when he was getting on to 70 in 484 BC. At first, both Duke Ai and Ji Kang consulted him on political principles. Unfortunately, however, the ideal governance that Confucius pursued was not on the same track with the practical self-serving politics. Confucius could not engage in the practical politics; nevertheless, he had never shifted his attention. In his later years, he focused his primary attention on education, which, to him, would mean a different way of engaging in politics if only that could generate impacts on politics. After his decade-long trekking among the states and observation, he came to realize that to engage in politics one did not necessarily have to sit behind an official table.

After his return to the State of Lu, Confucius edited the *Spring and Autumn Annals* and compiled the popular poetry and songs of his time. It was his efforts in compilation and promotion that made the *Book of Songs* acquire currency, leaving a precious cultural heritage to later ages.

In 479 BC, Confucius passed away from illness at the age of 73.

Zhu Xi, a renowned philosopher and educator in the Southern Song Dynasty, once remarked Confucius' status in history with a poem, two lines of which read "Had Confucius not been born, /We will forever live in an interminable night." In spite of the palpable hyperbole in the poem, we can detect the enormous contributions Confucius has made to Chinese culture. There has been no one comparable to Confucius in casting such a profound influence on the Chinese cultural-psychological structure. Apart from the conservative tinges, the teachings of Confucius featuring profound sophistication contributed to the social progress of his time and got further developed in the Warring States Period to be one of the distinguished schools of thought of the pre-Qin era. Due to historical reasons, his teachings did not receive much due attention from the ruling class until the Han Dynasty.

From the Han Dynasty onward, centralization of government dominated the feudal rule. Confucian teachings turned out to be serving the needs of the ruling class and won their attention. By the time of Emperor Wu of the Han Dynasty who adopted the proposal of counselor Dong Zhongshu to "pay supreme tribute to Confucianism while banning all other schools of thought", the ruling status of Confucius and his teachings in Chinese ideology had been established. Thereafter, the supreme status of Confucius was further cemented by generations of rulers through deifying him and advocating his doctrines, which, in turn, cast tremendous influence on philosophy, literature, art, education, and histography of the feudal China. Furthermore, as a leading representative of traditional Chinese culture, such an influence permeated the whole of eastern Asia and even the rest of the world. During the long period of feudal society, however, the conservative facets of his doctrines were magnified to serve the needs of the ruling class, and fettered people's mind.

Ever since the May 4th Movement, the conservatism of Confucian doctrines has been criticized by the progressive thinkers. Today's scholars are trying to evaluate and interpret Confucius and his doctrines by increasingly objective approaches with full reference to the historical backgrounds. It goes without saying that many of his doctrines are still showing deep impact on the modern society: human-based benevolence, human values, moral principles, primary importance of peace, global unity, unity of man and heaven, the harmony among human beings and between man and nature, and even his contented predestinarianism.

art, education, and historiography of the feudal China. Furthermore, as a leading representative of traditional Chinese culture, such an influence permeated the whole of eastern Asia and even the rest of the world. During the long period of feudal society, however, the conservative facets of his doctrines were magnified to serve the needs of the ruling class, and fettered people's mind.

Ever since the May 4th Movement, the conservatism of Confucian doctrines has been criticized by the progressive thinkers. Today's scholars are trying to evaluate and interpret Confucius and his doctrines by increasingly objective approaches with full reference to the historical backgrounds. It goes without saying that many of his doctrines are still showing deep impact on the modern society: human-based benevolence, human values, moral principles, primary importance of peace, global unity, unity of man and heaven, the harmony among human beings and between man and nature, and even his centemed predestinarianism.

孔子智慧故事
Wisdom of Confucius

1. 孔子学琴

孔子曾跟随鲁国的音乐家师襄子学弹琴。学了十天了，师襄子说："你可以学新乐曲了。"孔子摇摇头："不行，不行，我才学会了曲子，节奏还把握得不太准确。"又过了些时候，师襄子说："可以了，你现在节奏已经掌握准确了，可以学新的了。"孔子又摇摇头说："不行不行，我还没有领会乐曲的主题。"孔子继续操练同一首曲子。师襄子又等待了一段日子，说："现在主题也把握了，可以学习新曲子了。"孔子仍旧摇头，说："还不行，我觉得自己还没有深刻地理解作者本人。"这样，很长时间过去了，终于有一天，孔子说："现在我琢磨出来了，作者是一个思想深邃的人，是一个乐观的人，是一个眼光远大的人，这个人好像是个王者。莫非他就是周文王？如果不是他，又有谁还能作出这样的歌曲呢？"师襄子听他这样说，不由得恭恭敬敬地站起身来，佩服地说："是啊，我们老师教我们的时候也说这些乐章相传是周文王作的《文王操》。”

下工夫虚心而踏实地学习，应该是学生的本分。能否潜下心来学习，是否对所学的内容投入感情，都关系到学习的成败。而这样反反复复地探索玩味同一部作品，由表及里，从作品到作者，细细品味，力求把握作者的本意，而不是随意曲解，牵强附会，应该是我们阅读作品、欣赏作品的基础。

LEARNING TO PLAY THE *QIN*

Confucius once followed the well-known Shi Xiangzi in the State of Lu to play the *qin*, a type of ancient stringed musical instrument. 10 days had passed, Shi Xiangzi said to Confucius, "Now you can turn to a new piece." Shaking his head, Confucius said, "No, I can't! I have just learned how to play the music, but have not mastered the beats yet." Some time later, Shi Xiangzi said, "Now you've got the right beat, and you can pick up a new one." Shaking his head again, Confucius said, "No, I can't. I have not quite grasped the theme yet." Confucius went on with the same music. Quite some time had passed, and Shi Xiangzi asked Confucius, "Now you've grasped the theme. Shall we move on to a new one?" Confucius, however, said, "Not yet! I have not quite understood the composer."

A long time had passed. One day, Confucius finally said, "Now I have come to understand that the composer must be one with profound thoughts, optimistic mind, and great ambition. It seems that he is a king. Isn't he the King Wen of Zhou? Were it not him, who else could have composed such a masterpiece?" At this, Shi Xiangzi straightened his body in reverence, "There you go! When my mentor taught it to us, he also said that such pieces were believed to be the

Chant of King Wen composed by King Wen!"

It is the students' duty to learn with a modest heart and solid steps. The concentration of time and feelings plays an important role in one's learning. To read and appreciate literary works, one should relish on the same piece like Confucius, from the surface to the center, from the works to the composer, so as to grasp the essence, rather than take things for granted and draw far-fetched conclusions.

2. 什么是立国之本

孔子的学生子贡问，“治理一个国家，最需要什么呢？”孔子的回答很简单，“足食，足兵，民信之矣。”他说首先要有足够的粮食，老百姓能够丰衣足食。其次国家要强大，要有足够的军备做保障。有了这两条，百姓对国家就有信心了。

子贡又问，“如果没有办法同时一下子具备这三条，在粮食、军备和人民的信心三者中不得不去掉一项，那先去掉哪一项？”孔子说，“去掉军备。”

子贡接着问，“如果还是没有办法一下子既具备充足的粮食又赢得人民的信心，那么又该先去掉哪一项呢？”孔子说，“去掉粮食。”

子贡觉得奇怪，“没有了吃的，不是马上就饿死了吗？那怎么办？”

孔子又作了解释，“没有吃的，人是要饿死。但是自古以来，人都是免不了要死的。可是，如果人民对国家失去信心，这个国家就不能立国。即便吃的粮食再充足，得不到人民信任的国家还是站不起来的，持续不下去的。”

历史上无数的事实为孔子的回答作了注解。物质生活固然重要，然而人民的精神世界是更需要执政者关注的。只要大家心往一处想，劲儿往一处使，那么再大的困难也可以战胜。天灾人祸造成的饥荒会在人民的齐心协力面前退却；而一旦民心涣散，即便人人锦衣玉食，国家也很快就会分崩离析。至于军备的扩张，更是每个国家都应该首先放弃的。倘若各国和平共处，世界大同，国富民安，长枪短炮又有什么用处呢？

THE ESSENTIALS TO GOVERN A STATE

Zi Gong asked Confucius what were the essentials to govern a state. Confucius answered simply, "Sufficient food, sufficient arms, and people's faith." Confucius believed that primarily sufficient food was the premise for the people to be well-fed and clothed. Then sufficient arms could ensure a strong state. With these two guaranteed, the people would have faith in their state.

Zi Gong went on asking, "What if it was hard to meet all the three prerequisites, and one had to be given up, then which one first?" Confucius said, "It was the arms."

Zi Gong continued, "What if it was still hard to secure sufficient food and people's faith, and one had to be given up, then which one first?" Confucius said, "It was food."

Zi Gong felt surprised, "Without food one would soon starve to death. What then?"

Confucius admitted, "People could starve without food. But people die at all times. If the people, however, had lost their faith in the state, the state would soon die. However sufficient food there was, a state would not last long without people's faith."

Numerous facts in history have footnoted Confucius' views. The material life is indeed very important, but the mental state of the people should be of primary concern by the rulers. If all sharing the same goal and with concerted efforts, they will overcome any difficulties. United people could defeat famine caused by natural or man-made calamities. When people are not of one mind, a state will soon disintegrate, however good food and clothes its people have. Military expansion, especially, should be abandoned for every state. Providing all states co-exist in peace and harmony, and their people are well-fed, what use can the guns and cannons have?

3. 安贫乐道

颜回是孔子的得意门生之一，孔子曾经这样夸奖他："颜回的品质是多么高尚啊！一箪饭，一瓢水，住在简陋的小屋里，别人都忍受不了这种穷困清苦，颜回却没有改变他好学的乐趣。颜回的品质是多么高尚啊！"颜回是穷人家的孩子，住在简陋的小巷子里，一点饭，一点水，也生活得很快乐。如果别人这样过日子，一定发愁郁闷，而颜回却还是积极乐观地生活，没有哀叹抱怨，保持着内心的恬淡与安宁。这样的人，孔子称赞他是一个"贤者"，一个有着高度修养的人。

"一箪一瓢"即一只盛饭的竹筐，一个盛水的瓜瓢，以后就成了清贫生活的代名词。事实上孔子自己也从不为贫困所困。他曾经说过，"吃粗食，喝清水，弯起胳膊当枕头，也是快乐的生活。如果用不正当的手段来谋取富贵，对我来说就像天上的浮云一样。"这种贫困的生活，对于孔颜二人来说，一样充满乐趣，而且贫困的时间再长，也不会丧失其中的乐趣。一个人快乐与否，并不取决于物质生活，而是取决于个人的志趣与心态。

当然，如果能够改变贫困的生活，过上富裕舒适的日子，自然是人人都希望的。只是这种改变应该是合法、合理、合情的。所以孔子铿锵有力地说："发大财，做大官，这是人人都盼望的。如果不是用正当的方法得到的，君子不会接受；穷困和下贱，这是人人都厌恶的。如果不用正当的方法摆脱它，君子也不会去掉它。"

SIMPLE LIVING AND HIGH THINKING

Yan Hui was one of Confucius' favorite disciples. Confucius once praised him, "How admirable Yan Hui is! A bowlful of rice to eat, a gourdful of water to drink, and living in a mean dwelling; all these are hardships others would find intolerable, but Yan Hui does not allow them to affect his joy of learning. How admirable Yan Hui is!"

Born in poverty, Yan Hui dwelled in a tatty lane with some rice and water, but enjoyed himself. Such a life would surely frustrate others, but not Yan Hui who was optimistic without complaints. He kept his internal peace and tranquility. Confucius praised him as a "virtuous man", one that was highly cultivated.

"A bowlful of rice and a gourdful of water" referred to a bamboo bowl and a gourd water container, which have become a metaphor for poor life. In fact, Confucius himself was never disturbed by poverty. He once remarked, "There is happiness in eating coarse food and drinking plain water, and sleeping with a bent elbow as a pillow. Wealth and high position won in an immoral way are like floating clouds to me." Such a poor life held joys for Confucius and Yan Hui, and the joys were not to erode however long the poor life lasted. One's joys are not dependent on material life, but his interest and the state of mind.

Surely, it is the universal wish to shake off poverty and live a comfortable life, but through reasonable means. Thus Confucius emphasized forcefully, "Everyone wishes for fame and gain, but gentlemen will distain them if they are achieved in a wrong way. Everyone hates poverty and lowliness, but gentlemen will not shake them off if by unfair means."

4. 君子固穷

公元前 489 年，吴国进攻陈国。当时孔子恰好带着弟子们住在陈国。因为楚国帮助陈国，又听说楚王开明，而楚王也敬佩孔子的为人，希望孔子到楚国去，孔子就同意了。路上，他们正好经过一处吴楚作战的地方，吴蔡两国的大夫不愿让孔子为楚国所用，就把孔子和他的弟子们围住了，一连数日没让脱身。这时他们带的粮食吃光了。随行的弟子们劳累加上饥饿，有些就病倒了。直性子的子路很不高兴地去见孔子，问："有道德、有学问的君子也有这么遭难落魄的时候吗？"孔子心平气和地回答他说："有道德、有学问的君子当然也会遇到有难处的时候，但他不会因为遭了难而改变气节。没有道德、没有学问的小人一旦遭遇这样的困难，就会为自己找到好的路子而失去操守，没有节制，为所欲为。"

事实上，君子会比常人更多地遭遇到困境，因为君子坚持道德的操守，坚定不移，决不跟人同流合污，不会昧着良心说话，不会昧着良心做事，不会投人所好，在政治不清、人心不善的年代就会陷入困境，甚至至死不得解脱。东汉陶渊明曾经在《饮酒·其二》中写道："不赖固穷节，百世当谁传。"历史证明，流芳百世的只有君子，是那些为理想、为正道陷入困境，不为困境压倒的仁人志士。孔子说的"岁寒，然后知松柏之后凋也"千百年来激励了多少为正义赴汤蹈火的仁人义士！"君子不会片刻离开仁德，即便只是吃一顿饭的时间；在仓促匆忙的时候和仁德同在，在颠沛流离的时候也一定和仁德同在。"仁德应该成为每个人心头的明灯，在感觉黑暗的时候，用它来寻找光明。

A GENTLEMAN IS FIRM IN ADVERSITY

In 489 BC, the State of Wu attacked the State of Chen, where Confucius lived with some of his disciples at the time. The State of Chu had offered to come to Chen's rescue. It was said that the king of Chu was open-minded and rather admired Confucius. Thus Confucius readily accepted the invitation from the king of Chu to visit. On their way, Confucius and his disciples passed a battlefield between Wu and Chu. The senior ministers from the states of Wu and Cai would not let Confucius serve Chu and had Confucius and his disciples caught in besiegement for several days. They soon ran out of provisions. Exhausted and starving, some of his men fell ill.

The straightforward Zi Lu, with dissatisfaction written all over his face, said, "Are there times when even gentlemen of great learning and virtues are brought to such straits?" In a placid mood Confucius told him, "It comes as no surprise that a gentleman of great learning and virtues finds himself in dire straits; he will still uphold his morals and ethics. A small man finding himself in dire straits would throw over all restraints for what he has available."

Actually, gentlemen would encounter more straits than ordinary people. That's because they hold to their moral principles, and never join any bad company. They always speak and act out of their conscience, but never cater to other's unjustified pleasures. Therefore, in times of political disorder and confusion, such gentlemen would easily face a wretched plight — some could even get caught until death.

Tao Yuanming, the noted poet of the Eastern Han Dynasty, wrote in his *Poem Drinking Wine*: "Had he not dared to be poor and feel no shame/ How can he have preserved his timeless fame?" As history has long proved, it has been those who do not succumb to hardships while in pursuit of their ideals or just causes that could have a niche in the hall of fame. As Confucius had remarked, "Only in cold winter does one know that the pines and cypresses are the last to shed." It has inspired generations of heroes in their fight for justice. "Be it in a haste or in destitution, a gentleman will not put aside his virtues even for the time of a meal." Moral virtues should be a bright lamp shining in the heart of everyone, a lamp that will guide one through darkness for the lights.

5. 改变还是坚守?

在陈国去往楚国的路上被困在战乱中绝粮的时候，孔子知道弟子们心中有忧愁疑虑，便把子路叫来，问他：“《诗》中说，‘不是犀牛，不是老虎，奔走于旷野之间，是何缘由？’我们现在的处境，是不是因为我们的学说不正确？否则为何沦落在这个地方。”子路说：“可能是我们的仁德还不够，所以别人不信任我们；可能是我们的智慧还不够，所以别人不采用我们的主张。”“子路啊，要是有仁德就能让人信任，伯夷叔齐怎么会饿死在首阳山？要是有智慧就能推行自己的主张，比干怎么会被剖了心而死去？”孔子叫着子路的名字这样说。

子路走后，孔子又叫了子贡来问他同样的问题。子贡说：“老师的学说太深远、太宏大，所以很难被别人理解，让天下人接受。老师您是不是可以降低一下标准呢？”“子贡啊，要知道，一个优秀的农夫善于耕耘、长于播种，却不一定能获得好收成；一个优秀的工匠有灵巧的双手做出好东西，却不一定能迎合别人的喜好；一个君子有条理清晰的学说，却不一定能被世人接受。你怎么可以不谋求自己学说进一步的发展，转而去求得别人的接纳呢？你这样的志向太不高远了。”孔子又批评了子贡。

子贡走后，颜回来见孔子。孔子还是问他同一个问题。颜回说：“老师您的学说深远，因此不被人接受。即便如此，您仍然坚持推行自己的学说，不被接受又怎样呢？不被接受不被容纳，才能考验君子的本色。学说不完善，可耻的是我们；而完善的学说不被接受，可耻的却是执政者。不被接受又如何？不被接受才能考验君子的本色。”听到颜回这样说，孔子十分开心，笑眯眯地对颜回说：“是这个道理啊，颜氏之子。假如你发了财，我愿给你做管家。”

孔子很高兴颜回这么理解他，也用颜回的这种理解让大家来理解当时的处境。他同时也派子贡去和楚军交涉，楚昭王派了军队来迎接孔子，一行人终于得以脱离困境。

在任何压力下不动摇自己的主张，不降低理想的标准，坚持走自己的路，需要信念，需要勇气，也需要别人的理解。怀有相同信念的人手牵手一起走，坎坷的路就容易踩平。

TO CHANGE OR TO PERSEVERE?

Having got trapped on the battlefield and running out of provisions while on the way from the State of Chen to the State of Chu, Confucius knew his disciples had worries and complaints. He summoned Zi Lu to his front and asked, “In *The Book of Odes* it reads, ‘It is neither a tiger nor a rhinoceros, but keeps running around in the wild field. Why bother?’ See how we are caught in such straits! Is it because our doctrines are not correct? Or why could we have got caught?” To that Zi Lu said, "It may be that our benevolence has not been enough yet, and people do not trust us; or that our wisdom is not sufficient, and people do not accept our proposals." "But, Zi Lu!" Confucius said, "Were it in benevolence that trust lies, why should have Bo Yi and Shu Qi starved in Mount Shouyang? Were it on wisdom that our proposals depend, why should have Bi Gan's heart got cut?"

After Zi Lu walked away, Confucius summoned Zi Gong and asked him the same question. To that Zi Gong said, "It may be that your doctrines are too profound and deep for people to understand or accept. Master, would you think to tune down your criteria a bit?" "But, Zi Gong!" Confucius blamed him, "A good farmer is good at plowing and sowing, but may not reap a good harvest. An excellent craftsman has skillful hands to create masterpieces, but may not meet other's tastes. A gentleman has well-reasoned doctrines, but may not be accepted by people. How could you not aim to improve your own doctrines, but to seek people's acceptance? As such, you do not have a high ambition!"

After Zi Gong walked away, Confucius summoned Yan Hui and asked him the same question. To that Yan Hui said, "Master, your doctrines cannot be accepted because of their profoundness. Even now, you persevere to promote your doctrines. Why bother if they are not yet accepted? When one is not accepted, the true colors of a gentleman are put to the test. If it is because our doctrines are not complete, the shame should be on us. If it is our complete doctrines that are not accepted, the shame is on the rulers. Why bother if they are not accepted? When they are not accepted, the true colors of a gentleman are put to the test." At this, Confucius smiled with joy, "Just it, my son! When you are wealthy, I would love to be your housekeeper."

Confucius was so pleased because Yan Hui could so understand him, and let other disciples understand the situation with Yan Hui's example. Meanwhile, he sent Zi Gong to negotiate with the Chu Army. Eventually, King Zhao of Chu dispatched his troops to welcome Confucius. He and his followers finally got out of the straits.

It requires faith, courage, and understanding from others for one to stand firm with his views, not to scale down his criteria, and to persevere on his own way. Should those sharing the same faith join their hands, they will overcome difficulties easily.

6. 贫与富

子贡问老师："假如一个人贫穷而不向富人谄媚，假如一个人富有而不盛气凌人，这样的人怎么样？"

孔子说："这样的人还可以，但还不够。如果他贫穷却依然乐于道，富有却依旧谦逊有礼，那就更好了。"

子贡通过做生意成了有钱人，他向老师提出了穷人和富人的做人的标准。从一般人的角度来看，子贡的想法已经很不错，是比较高的要求了，但孔子提出了更高的境界。穷人不仅能够对富人不阿谀奉承讨好迎合，还要能够忧道不忧贫；富人不仅能够不骄奢摆谱，还要能够彬彬有礼不逾规矩。为什么这么说？因为孔子觉察到了人性的弱点，或者人穷志短，品德气节终被抛弃；或者财大气粗，随心所欲，胡作非为。

所以电影《简·爱》中平民女子简·爱对富贵公爵罗切斯特所说

的那句掷地有声的台词："我们的精神是同等的！就如同你跟我经过坟墓将同样地站在上帝面前！"至今赢得世人的喜爱。

POOR AND RICH

Zi Gong once asked Confucius, "One is poor but does not flatter the rich. One is rich but does not bully others. What would become of such people?"

Confucius said, "Such people are pretty good, but not good enough. It will be perfect if he is poor but devotes himself to virtues, or if he is rich but retaining modesty."

Zi Gong became rich through his business. He asked Confucius on the criteria of behaviors for the poor and the rich. By a general standard, Zi Gong was quite remarkable with his criteria. But Confucius proposed a higher level of judgment. Being poor, one needs not only flatter not the rich but remain concerned on moral virtues rather than poverty. Being rich, one needs not only bully not the poor, but also remain courteous with proprieties. Why so? Obviously, Confucius had detected the weakness in human nature. Some run out of ambitions when they are poor, and they eventually desert moral virtues. Some run out of proprieties when they are rich, and behave willfully.

This also explains the lasting popularity of what the commoner Jane Eyre said in face of Lord Rochester in the movie: "It is my spirit that addresses your spirit; just as if both had passed through the grave, and we stood at God's feet, equal — as we are!"

7. 己所不欲，勿施于人

子贡问了孔子一个非常大的问题："有没有一个字就可以拿来终身实践的呢？"

孔子说："那就是恕吧！"什么是"恕"呢？老师又加了八个字的解释，叫做"己所不欲，勿施于人"，就是一个人自己不想要的，就不要强迫别人要。比如说你不想被别人打，那么你就不要去打别人；你不想别人损害你的利益，那么你也就不要去损害别人的利益；你不想别人干涉你的自由，那么你也不要去干涉别人的自由。这是作为人的教养，也是人的文化。这种文化是人类区别于动物的特征之一，因此，在东西方文明中，这样的准则其实是普遍的。在印度史诗《摩诃婆罗多》中说到："你自己不想经受的事，不要对别人做；你自己向往渴求的事，也该希望别人得到——这就是全部的律法，留心遵行吧。"《圣经·马太福音》中说："你们要别人怎样对待你们，就得怎样对待别人

——这就是摩西律法和先知教训的真义。”

“己所不欲，勿施于人”这一孔子的名言指的是自己不想要的东西，切勿强加给别人。这是一种用否定方式表现的推己及人，可以称之为恕。推己及人的另一种表现是积极的，用孔子的话说是“己欲立而立人，己欲达而达人”，可以称之为忠。推己及人的这两个方面合在一起，就叫做忠恕之道，是实行仁的两大方法。因为孔子学说的核心是仁爱，所以我们就可以理解《论语》中的“夫子之道，忠恕而已矣”的提法。

REFRAINING FROM IMPOSING UNDESIRABLE THINGS ON OTHERS

Once Zi Gong raised a big issue to Confucius, "Is there a word which may serve as a rule of practice for all one's life?"

Confucius said, "Perhaps it is reciprocity!" Then he added his interpretation: "Do not impose on others what you do not desire yourself." For instance, if you do not want a beat, do not beat others; if you do not want your benefits to be hurt, do not hurt others'; if you do not want your freedom to be interfered with, do not interfere with the freedom of others. Actually this is one of the basic features that reflect the cultivation and culture of the human beings, and that distinguishes human beings from animals.

As a matter of fact, there is such a golden rule in both the oriental and the occidental cultures. In the Indian epic *Mahabharata* it reads, "This is the sum of duty: do naught unto others which would cause you pain if done to you." Similarly in the *Gospel of Matthew* in the *Bible* it reads, "All things whatsoever ye would that men should do to you, do ye even so to them: for this is the law and the prophets."

The Confucian version of the golden rule means one should not impose on others what oneself favors not. Confucius approached the issue from an empathetic, disaffirmative perspective, which is called reciprocity. The Confucius' empathy has an affirmative perspective, which is called loyalty, or to quote Confucius, "Helping others to be established when one wishes to be established himself, and helping others to be successful when one wishes to be successful himself." The two perspectives of such empathy combined are loyalty and reciprocity, two principal means of practicing benevolence. Since benevolence lies in the very core of Confucius' doctrines, we therefore can understand "Our Master's Way, loyalty and reciprocity, this and nothing more" in *The Analects*.

8. 名正言顺

在卫灵公做卫国国君的时候，孔子曾经在卫国住过，还见过卫灵公的夫人南子。南子是个妩媚而轻浮的女人，却深得卫灵公的宠爱。有一次南子一定要见见孔子，孔子拒绝不了，不得不去见她。后来又被卫灵公和南子一起邀请一同坐车出门，孔子很难堪，却也没有办法。子路对老师的做法不满意，觉得有些失身份，因为卫灵公不理朝政，只与南子、宠臣等鬼混，名声不好。甚至卫灵公的儿子蒯聩都想杀死有淫乱名声的母亲，但没有成功，反而被卫灵公赶出了卫国。卫灵公死后，继承王位的卫出公是他的孙子，也就是蒯聩的儿子辄，而且辄还拒绝父亲回国继位。因为卫灵公没有重用过孔子，而卫出公和逃亡在外的父亲又发生了剧烈的内部斗争，孔子因此离开了卫国。那是孔子60岁那年。又过了三年，卫出公在位三年，国家基本稳定，孔子的弟子中也有在卫国做事的，卫出公来请孔子担任重要职务。这时，孔子的学生子路问孔子:“卫国国君正等待您去辅助他治理国事,不知道您准备从哪一方面开始?”孔子说:“那一定要从端正名分开始。”子路很吃惊,“您真是迂腐,这名分怎么正?正它干什么?”

孔子听了,非常生气。“你怎么这么说呢!太鲁莽了。仲由,作为一个君子,对于自己不懂的事情要采取存疑的态度,暂时放一边不要谈。你要知道,如果名分不正,说起话来理就不顺;说话理不顺,做事就不会成功;做事不能成功,礼乐教化就不能兴盛;礼乐教化不能兴盛,刑罚也就不会得当;刑罚不得当,百姓就不能安生,就像手脚都不知道该放在哪儿。所以君子确定一个名分就一定要准确,有他的理由。言之有理了,就一定能做到。君子对自己说的话,可不能随随便便。”

孔子是提倡“君君臣臣父父子子”的,希望君臣父子都应该在自己的名分下说话做事,不可以乱了规矩。而卫灵公做国君的时候不好好治理国政,蒯聩作为儿子却想杀死自己的母亲,而辄又不让自己的父亲回国;蒯聩当时只是一个臣子,又要去夺取君王的位子,所以这祖孙三代,都是君王不像君王,父亲不像父亲,儿子不像儿子,臣子也不像臣子。一个国家的上层都这么混乱,平民百姓怎么能够安居乐业?所以孔子认为正名分是一件十分重要、首先得做的事情。如果一个盛酒的器皿叫“觚”,却没有两只角,那就不是“觚”。

孔子所说的这个正名,是跟古代礼制有关的,是和伦理政治有关的,不是一般语言修辞上的用语准确与否。但由此流传下来的这个词语“名正言顺”,却有了更广泛的用途。因为“名义正当,道理讲得通”就可以做。不过,孔子的正名有它的特点,他要求具体的事物要符合名为它所限定的含义,就像穿鞋子,如果鞋子太小了,不是在鞋子上想办法,而是削足适履,这一思想受到不少人的异议。

THE RIGHT NAME FOR PROPER WORDS

During the reign of Duke Ling, Confucius once lived in the State of Wei and even met the duchess Nanzi, who was charming but frivolous and much favored by the duke. Nanzi once insisted to give audience to Confucius and he found no way to decline. Some time later, Confucius was invited by the duke and his duchess to ride their carriage. Confucius felt extremely awkward but again could find no way to decline. Much dissatisfied, Zi Lu felt it was beneath his master's dignity as the duke had such a bad fame of hanging around with his duchess and minions while neglecting his court duties. Even the duke's son Kuai Kui attempted to assassinate his licentious mother, but he failed and was banished out of Wei. After the death of Duke Ling, the throne was succeeded by his grandson Kuai Zhe. Kuai Zhe, Duke Chu, was the son of Kuai Kui, and refused to let his father return for the throne.

As Confucius had never received any serious attention from Duke Ling, plus now the new Duke Chu was in fierce conflicts with his banished father, Confucius left the State of Wei at the age of 60. Three years later, the State of Wei resumed some stability after Duke Chu's three-year ruling. Besides, some of Confucius' disciples were serving in Wei. Duke Chu then extended a big offer to Confucius to return. His disciple Zi Lu asked, "Master, the duke of Wei is awaiting you to assist his governance. Where would you start with?" To that Confucius said, "What is necessary is to rectify names." Puzzled, Zi Lu asked, "Why so stubborn? Why must there be such rectification?"

Rather annoyed, Confucius retorted his disciple, "How rude you are, Zhong You! A gentleman avoids making comments on things he does not know. When the name is not instituted properly, instructions will not be accepted; when instructions are not accepted, work is not accomplished; when work is not accomplished, rites and music cannot thrive. Rites and music cannot thrive, punishment and penalties are not carried out properly; punishment and penalties are not carried out properly, then the commoners cannot live in peace. Thus a gentleman needs a proper name to instruct properly and take due actions. What a gentleman says is but earnest."

Confucius proposed to "let the king be a king, the minister a minister, the father a father, and the son a son." He advocated that the king and the minister, the father and the son should behave properly under their respective names and should not break the rules. However, Duke Ling had not ruled properly. As a son, Kuai Kui attempted to kill his own mother and refused to let his father back. As an official, he attempted to usurp the throne. The father, the son, the grandson — none of the three generations had behaved properly. When the rulers of a state fell into such disorder, how could the commoners live in peace? Thus Confucius insisted that it be a mission of primary significance to rectify the names. It is just like a *gu* that holds wine. If that *gu* does not have the two handles, it is hardly a *gu* any more.

Confucius' theory of rectification had a bearing on the ancient rituals and ethical politics rather than in the sense of general rhetorical purposes. As an expression, "the right name for proper words" has come down from Confucius but gained wider usage. When the name is justified, instructions can be accepted and things can be accomplished. Whereas Confucius had a different definition to the "right name" as he required a specific object to fit its preset definition. It was like to require one to cut his feet to fit the shoes if the shoes were too small. And such a thought had invited much criticism.

9. 人若无信

春秋时期，吴王寿梦有四个儿子，第四个儿子最贤能，叫季札。季札出使各国的时候，经过徐国，徐国国君看到季札身佩的宝剑十分喜欢，但不好意思说出口向季札索要。季札其实已经看出来了，但因为身负出使别国的重任，使臣又不能不佩剑，所以也没说什么，可是心里却暗暗答应徐国国君等出使返回后要把佩剑送给他。后来季札又到了徐国，徐国国君却已经去世了。季札便把宝剑解下来，挂在徐国国君墓旁的树上。有人说："人都死了，你干吗还要把宝剑送给他啊。"季札回答："我在心里答应过他的，不能因为他死了就变了心。"这个讲信义的季札是孔子非常敬重的。孔子说："一个人要是没有信用，就不知道他能干什么了。大车没有輗（ní,大车车辕上的销钉），小车没有軏（yuè,小车车辕上的销钉），那还怎么动得了？"

孔子提出了"信"这个重要的道德观念。交朋友，要以信为基础；

经商，要以信为本；为政，也必须获得人民的信任。把诚信看做是一个人、一个国家、一个民族安身立命的根基，成了后来许多人的共识。两千年前的《吕氏春秋》里有《贵信》一篇，大意说，如果君臣互相不讲诚信，那么老百姓之间就会互相诽谤，国家就不得安宁；做官的不讲诚信，那么年少的就不会敬畏年长的，有地位的没地位的相互鄙视；奖赏惩罚制度没有诚信，那么民众就容易犯法，无法管理他们；交朋友的时候如果没有诚信，那么就会心生怨言，不能亲近，只会分离；各行业的工匠如果没有诚信，那么做出来的东西就会是假的，上的油漆染的颜色都不会牢固。现代思想家陈独秀也认为，人类如果不讲诚信，不单单是道德的羞耻，还会成为经济的拖累。可以说，孔子、吕不韦、陈独秀说的都是一个道理。

FAITH

During the Spring and Autumn Period, King Mengshou of the State of Wu had 4 sons, among whom the youngest, Ji Zha, was the most talented and virtuous. Ji Zha once served as an envoy to the states. When he was in the State of Xu, the king caught sight of Ji Zha's sword and showed explicit interest but rather hesitant to ask for it. Having read the king's mind, Ji Zha silently promised the gift after his trip as he needed the ritual sword to continue his mission.

Unfortunately, when Ji Zha returned to Xu, the king had passed away. Ji Zha released his sword and hung it on the tree beside the king's mausoleum. People asked Ji Zha why he should do that to one who had been dead. To that Ji Zha said he was living up to his faith, and he had no reason to change just because the king was dead. Confucius admired Ji Zha for his belief that one without faith would have little to accomplish. Likewise, a large cart without a pin in the yoke-bar or a small cart without a collar bar could not move.

Confucius made "faith" a cardinal moral virtue, which lied at the base of all things — making friends, doing business, governance to win people's trust. It was the very root of an individual, a country, or a nation. It too had been commonly acknowledged through the history. Similar views appeared in the *Value of Faith* in *Spring and Autumn of Master Lü Buwei* over two millennia ago. Were there no faith between the king and his ministers, the state would be in a state of total chaos with its people slandering one another. Were there no faith among the officials, the seniors would not be revered by the juniors and those in power and those powerless would despise each other. Were there no faith in award and punishment, the commoners would easily break laws and be hard to be governed. Were there no faith in making friends, people would eventually desert each other with complaints. Were there no faith in the craftsmen of any trade, there would be fakes out of their hands — the paint might fall soon. The modern thinker Chen Duxiu held similar view that the lack of faith would mean not only a moral shame but a drag to economic growth. Obviously, faith is the shared theme in the views of Confucius, Lü Buwei, and Chen Duxiu.

10. 师徒的愿望

有一次，子路、颜回站在孔子旁边，大家一起聊天。孔子提了个话题，“大家来谈谈各自的愿望吧”。直性子的子路总是率先开口：“希望有好马好车，还要有好的裘皮大衣。如果有这些好东西，我肯定愿意跟朋友们分享，即便用旧了用坏了，我也不觉得遗憾。”颜回说：“我的愿望是不夸耀自己的长处，也不表白自己的功劳。”子路听完，迫不及待转而问孔子：“老师，让我们也听听您老人家的愿望吧。”孔子坦白地向弟子们说明了自己的想法：“我希望能让老年人生活安逸，让朋友们彼此信任，让年轻人得到关怀。”

三人各不相同的愿望，很鲜明地表明了三个人的性情和学问。子路看重物质生活的享受，是喜欢结交朋友、重朋友情义的粗汉子。后来的文人们常用“鹿裘共弊、同袍还共弊、故人共弊”等来描写朋友之间的亲密无间。颜回比较重视精神修养，对自己要求严格。但这样的要求在现代社会，似乎已经很不合时宜。如果你不夸自己，那是你缺乏自信；如果你不表功，那是你缺乏政绩。孔子毕竟是老师，他的愿望充满温暖，充满仁爱。如果老人的生活安稳幸福，友人们诚信无欺，年轻人有人关心管教，那么这个社会一定是处在太平盛世中。人们所渴望的尧舜时代，不过就是如此吧。而这正是孔子孜孜以求的理想社会。

DREAMS OF THE MASTER AND HIS DISCIPLES

Confucius was once chatting with Zi Lu and Yan Hui. Confucius raised a topic, asking them each to talk about their dreams. Straightforward as he was, Zi Lu was always the first to talk, "I wish that I could have a good carriage with strong steeds, and good fur coats. Then I would share with my friends and have no regret when they are damaged." Then Yan Hui said, "I would wish not to boast my strength and achievements." Impatient to wait, Zi Lu turned to Confucius asking, "Master, can we know what your dream is?" Freeheartedly, Confucius said, "I wish that the old could live in comfort, friends could have trust, and the young could be cared."

Different dreams of the three showed their different characters and scholarship. Unsophisticated as he was, Zi Lu had a taste for material comforts, making friends and enjoyed brotherhood, and fit the analogies for close friendship of later times like "sharing a fur coat", "sharing the same dress and shelter", "old friends sharing a shelter". Yan Hui, on the other hand, had his mind set for spiritual cultivation, and was strict with himself. However, that does not seem to fit the needs of our times. If one does not boast around, he shows a lack of confidence. If one does not make known his achievements, he is not regarded to have achieved anything in the post.

After all, Confucius' dream as a master teemed with warmth and benevolence. Should the old live in peace, friends enjoy faith, and the young be cared, it must be the very halcyon times that ancient kings of Yao and Shun had pursued. And that was the very ideal society Confucius had eagerly aspired.

11. 朽木粪墙

孔子的弟子宰予，言辞美好，说起话来娓娓动听。在孔子的众多弟子中，宰予是出名的伶牙俐齿。起初，孔子很喜欢这个弟子，以为他一定很有出息。可是不久，宰予暴露出懒惰的毛病。一天，孔子给弟子讲课，发现宰予没有来听课，就派弟子去找。一会儿，去找的弟子回来报告说，宰予在房里睡大觉。那个时代没有电灯，人们都是日出而作，日入而息，白天是读书人的黄金时光。宰予却大白天睡懒觉。听到这一消息，孔子大失所望，很生气地说："腐烂了的木头没法雕刻出东西，烂泥巴砌的墙没法粉刷。至于宰予嘛，还责备什么呢？也不值得责备了。"过了一阵子，又说："最初我看一个人，听到他说的话便相信他的行为。现在看来，我听了一个人的话，还要考察他的行为。是宰予让我改变了态度。"

孔子看到宰予大白天睡觉，批评他是腐朽的木头不值得雕刻，以后就有了中国的成语“朽木不可雕”，比喻人已经败坏到不可救药的地步。孔子认为宰予和子贡是最适合做外交官的，擅长辞令与外交应对。却没想到宰予是只说不做，所以孔子得到的经验是听其言还需观其行。判断一个人说的是否属实，一定要结合行动来共同考察。这个经验有普遍意义，涉及先秦时代关注的名实问题，以后的韩非子虽然属于法家，但也说要审核刑名，统治者考察臣下，不仅要看他怎么说的，更要看他是怎么做的；至于道家，则明确地说言辞华丽的不可信。

DECAYED WOOD AND DIRT

Confucius had a disciple named Zai Yu, who was good at words. His glibness and eloquence made him different from his fellow disciples. At first, Confucius favored him and pinned much hope on him. Soon after, however, Zai Yu showed his laziness. One day, Confucius found Zai Yu was absent from class, and sent someone to look for him and was then told that Zai Yu was still napping in his room.

At that time, there was no electricity. People rose and rest with the sun, and daytime had been more than precious to scholars. To his disappointment, Zai Yu was napping in the broad daylight. Confucius remarked in a rage, "Neither a piece of decayed wood nor a wall of dried dung can be turned into something beautiful. As such, what more can I ask from Zai Yu?" With a pause, Confucius continued, "I used to take a man at his words and trust he would act accordingly. But now after seeing Zai Yu, I judge a man by his words and deeds."

Zai Yu napped in the broad daylight, thus Confucius took him as a decayed wood that could not be carved, hence the Chinese saying "a decayed wood cannot be carved" to say someone as being worthless or hopeless. Confucius had thought Zai Yu and Zi Gong were good for diplomacy for their eloquence and reaction, but did not expect Zai Yu was only good at talks without action. Therefore, Confucius concluded that when he listened to a man's words he still needed to watch for his actions.

Such a view showed its universal significance that we need to review specific actions in making judgments of what one said. It reflected the emphasis on name and reality during the pre-Qin period. After that, Han Feizi, though a legalist, emphasized on examining the words and deeds, and the rulers needed to review what his ministers said but more what they did. As for Taoists, they had explicit expression on the incredibility of rhetoric.

12. 天下为什么会有贼

季康子是鲁国的高官，他问孔子治理国家的道理。孔子回答说："政这个字的意思就是正，中正。如果你能首先奉行正道，做臣民的表率，那么下层的人民，还有谁敢不走正道呢？"

后来季康子看着鲁国的盗贼很多，又问孔子怎样才能遏制盗窃的风气。孔子回答说："假如你们在上位的人本身很清廉，不贪婪，那么你即使奖赏人民去做盗贼，人民也不肯去做的。"

源清则流清，源浊则流浊，自古如此。《大学》里也说："尧舜时代用仁爱来统率天下，人民都跟着有仁有爱；桀纣时代用暴行来统率天下，人民都跟着使用暴力。"上行下效，统治者的一举一动，对人民的影响巨大。所以孔子向来主张所谓领袖，一定要以身作则，"为政以德"。如果执政者本身贪多求多，那么一定会想方设法横征暴敛，以满足私欲。人民在苛捐杂税下没有丰衣足食的可能，不想饿死冻死，就必定会沦为盗贼。相反，如果执政者廉洁奉公，真正做人民的衣食父母官，那就不会有多如牛毛的苛捐杂税，人民就会安居乐业。

WHY THERE ARE THIEVES?

Ji Kang, a senior official in the court of State Lu, once asked Confucius about governance. Confucius answered, "To govern means to be upright. If you are upright and take the lead for the commoners, who would dare not to be upright?"

Later on, seeing there were many thieves in Lu, Ji Kang went to Confucius asking how to curb. Confucius said, "If those who are ruling remain honest and free of corruption, people would not be thieves even though you provide a reward."

When the source of a stream is clear, the stream will be clear. When the source of a stream is muddy, the stream will be muddy. Such a truth has come down from history. *The Great Learning* echoed with similar views, "When rulers like Yao and Shun governed with benevolence, people showed benevolence and love. When rulers like Jie and Zhou ruled with tyranny, people resorted to violence." People follow the example of their superiors. Whatever the rulers do would exert tremendous influence on the people. Therefore, Confucius always advocated governance on virtues. When the rulers were greedy, they would tax the people to their bones. The people, in turn, would become thieves if they did not want to die in hunger or coldness. On the contrary, when the rulers were upright and honest to serve the people, there would not be endless taxes and the people could then live in peace.

13. 因人施教

孔子的学生常常喜欢问一些生活中遇到的问题。有一次，向来勇武的子路问老师："听到了就该去做吗？"孔子说："父亲和兄长都在，怎么可以听到了就去做！"向来温和的冉有也问老师："听到了就该去做吗？"孔子很干脆地回答："对，听到了就该去做！"在一旁听着的公西华觉得很奇怪，没了方向，这到底该做还是不该做。他忍不住问老师："子路问的是听到了该不该去做，老师说有父亲和兄长在；冉有问的也是听到了该不该去做，老师说听到了就该去做。我糊涂了，您为什么一会儿说不行一会儿说行，您能告诉我原因吗？"孔子的回答很简略："冉有平时做事总是犹豫不决，所以要鼓励他；子路做事总是胆大过人，所以要约束他。"

两个学生问了一个一模一样的问题，而老师的回答却是截然相反的。究其原因，是因为两个学生不同的个性。对鲁莽有余，细致不足的子路，老师告诫他要多征询父兄的意见，不要听风就是雨，要多想想。对温和有余，自信不足的冉有，老师敦促他要果断坚决，不要考虑再三还是做不出决定。学生个性不同，行为不同，老师能够用恰当的方式，让他的长处发扬光大，让他的短处日渐更正，这就是我们说的因人施教。《论语》中有很多这方面的例子。例如，“齐景公问政于孔子”，孔子的回答是“君君，臣臣，父父，子子”。子张问政，孔子的回答是“居之无倦，行之以忠”。而季康子问政，孔子的回答是“政者，正也；子帅以正，孰敢不正？”孔子的回答中一针见血地指出了不同人的弱点，从而达到修正的目的。

面向全体是当代教育的新理念，施教因人而异，承认、尊重教学对象的个体差异，是实现这一理念的必由之路。

TO TEACH ACCORDING TO INDIVIDUAL APTITUDE

Confucius' disciples often asked him about problems they met in their daily lives. Once the aggressive Zi Lu asked, "Should I take immediate action when I hear?" "You have your father and elder brothers," Confucius answered by saying, "How can you be in such haste?" Then the mild-mannered Ran You asked Confucius, "Should I take immediate action when I hear that something needs to be done?" "Yes, immediately!" Confucius told him. Rather puzzled, another disciple Gongxi Hua asked his Master, "When Zi Lu posed the question, you reminded him of his father and brothers. When Ran You posed the same question, you told him yes. Would you let me know the reason?" Confucius told him, "Ran You is always hesitant in making decisions, and he needs to be encouraged; while Zi Lu is always aggressive, and he needs to be restrained."

The two disciples asked the same question, but the Master's answers were different, because the two were of different aptitudes. Confucius warned the reckless Zi Lu to consult with his father and brothers and think twice before taking action. While for the mild but diffident Ran You, Confucius encouraged him to be decisive. When a teacher instructs the students according to their individual aptitudes, their merits could then be magnified while their flaws modified. That is to teach according to individual aptitudes. There are quite a few more cases in Confucius' *Analects* echoing such a view. In the *Duke Jing of the State of Qi Asking Confucius about Governance*, Confucius replied by saying, "Let the king be a king, the ministers be ministers, the father a father and the son a son." To the same question from Zi Zhang, Confucius answered by saying, "Concentrate fully on executing the task when in the position. When there is action to be taken, give it all your best." To Ji Kang, Confucius said, "To govern is to be upright. Who would dare not to be upright if you take the lead in being upright?" By answering in different ways, Confucius got to the right point to the individual weakness so as to help them rectify.

It is a new concept to provide every child with compulsory schooling in our time. To achieve that, it is crucial to recognize and respect individual differences in education.

14. 君子不偏向自己的儿子

陈亢是孔子的学生之一，不太出名，也可以算是孔子的儿子孔鲤的同学。他曾怀疑别的学生一定受到过孔子的特殊教导，比如孔子高足颜回，否则怎么会高出自己一筹呢？

有一天，陈亢问孔鲤："你在你父亲面前也听过什么特殊的教诲吗？"孔鲤很认真地回答说："没有啊！有一天他独自站在那里，我快步从庭中走过。他叫住我，问：'你学诗了没有？'我老实回答'没有'。'你不学诗，就没法跟别人交谈。'我回去后赶紧开始学诗。有一天他又独自站在那里，我快步从庭中走过。他又叫住我，问：'你学礼了没有？'我不敢骗他，乖乖地说：'没有。''你不学礼，就没有了立身的基础。'我回去后赶紧开始学礼。我就听过这两次。"

听了孔鲤的回答，陈亢很高兴，回去就跟人说："我问了一个问题，得到了三个收获：听到了学诗的作用，听到了学礼的作用，还知道了君子不偏向自己的儿子。”

君子不偏向自己的儿子，可以得到不少启示。如今的家长往往与孔子相反，把孩子的发展看做是一种竞争力，学习上要让孩子加班加点，唯恐别人家的孩子成绩超过自家的；生活上要事无巨细全部自己包揽，唯恐孩子吃苦受累；孩子犯了错，唯恐孩子受惩罚，自己走门路、跑关系，替孩子开脱。这样一来，有钱人家的孩子容易成为花花公子，有权人家的孩子是纨绔子弟，平常人家的孩子也往往心胸狭隘。如果像孔子一样，教导自己的孩子跟教导别人家的孩子一样，或者反过来说，教导别人家的孩子跟教导自己的孩子一样，那是一种多么可贵的精神。

A GENTLEMAN IS NEVER PARTIAL TO HIS SON

Chen Kang was Confucius' disciple. He did not acquire any big fame, except being a fellow disciple with Confucius' son Kong Li. Chen Kang was once suspicious that other fellow disciples must have received extra instructions from Confucius. Yan Hui, for instance, was among the favored. But how could he have achieved that?

One day, Chen Kang asked Kong Li: "As his son have you ever heard something different from what the rest of us hear?" Kong Li replied seriously saying, "No. Once when he was standing alone and I was hurrying past him across the courtyard, he said, 'Have you studied the *Songs*? I replied, 'No.' (He said) 'If you do not study the *Songs*, you will find yourself at a loss in conversation.' So I retreated and studied the *Songs*. Another day he was again standing alone, and as I hurried across the courtyard, he said, 'Have you studied the rites?' I replied, 'No.' (He said) 'If you do not study the rites, you will find yourself at a loss how to take your stand.' So I retreated and studied the rites. These are two things I heard from him."

Chen Kang came away delighted, saying, "I asked about one point, but got information about three. I learnt about the importance of the *Songs* and the rites, and also learnt that a gentleman keeps his son at a distance."

That a gentleman remains impartial to his son has been quite illuminating. Many parents today think differently from Confucius. They regard the development of their children as the way to compete, and impose on them extra work just in case that their children might fall behind their peers. In daily life the parents would take charge of all the work just in case that their children might suffer hardship. When the children have made mistakes, the parents would mobilize all their connections to avoid responsibilities. As a result, those in rich or powerful families might become dandies, those in poor families might become narrow minded. It is therefore of special value to educate one's own child in the same way as one would educate other's.

15. 孔子为何不隐世

楚国有两位隐士，一位叫长沮，一位叫桀溺。因为世道昏暗，他们就过起了隐居的生活。当孔子要离开楚国，准备取道蔡国回陈国的时候，看见两个农夫在一起耕田，这两个农夫就是隐居的长沮和桀溺。孔子一行想要渡河，却找不到渡口，孔子便让子路下车去向两个农夫问路。

长沮反问子路："那辆车上那个拿着缰绳的人是谁？"

子路说："是孔丘。"

长沮又问："就是鲁国的那位孔丘吗？"

子路说："是的。"

长沮于是说："他是周游列国的人，自然应该知道渡口在哪儿。"

子路见他不肯说，又去问桀溺。桀溺还是反问："你是谁？"

子路说："我是仲由。"

桀溺又问：“你就是鲁国孔丘的学生吗？”

子路回答说：“正是。”

于是，桀溺批评说：“如今世道混乱，就像那横流的洪水，到处泛滥，遍天下都是如此，谁能把它改变过来呢？而且孔丘到处与人意见不合，只好东奔西走，避开他人，你与其跟随像他那样的人，弄得徒劳无益，不如像我们这样，干脆避开世事，隐居起来，反倒清闲自在。”说完仍旧不停地平土播种再覆种，也不告诉子路哪里有渡口。

子路没有办法，不得不回去告诉孔子这两个农夫说的话。

孔子听了，心中有些怅然，自然也不高兴。他沉默了一会儿，感慨地说：“人总不能跟飞鸟走兽一起生活吧？如果我不跟这世上的人生活在一起，那还能跟谁生活在一起？如果天下已经清明太平，那我孔丘也就用不着这样东奔西走，试图改革了。”

孔子自己不隐世，他甚至还动员已经做了隐士的哲人像自己一样负起社会的责任。有一次，子路跟着孔子出去却落在后面走散了。子路遇见一位老人，老人用杖挑着一种竹器悠悠地走着。子路就上前问他：“您看见我的老师了吗？”老人说：“你是个四肢不劳作，五谷也分不清楚的人，我怎么知道谁是你的老师啊？”说完用手拄着拐杖，在田里除草。子路拱着手恭恭敬敬地站着等。老人见子路很有礼貌，便留他在家里住宿，并且杀鸡做饭招待他，又叫他两个儿子出来拜见。第二天，子路辞行，在找到孔子后告诉了老师经过的情形。孔子说：“这是一位隐士。”让子路再回到老人那里去拜见老人。可是等子路再到老人家的时候，老人已经外出了。子路只好把孔子交代的话转述给老人的家人：“一个人不替国家做事，就是废弃了君臣的大义。昨天老人让他的两个儿子出来相见，是因为长幼尊卑的礼节。老人知道长幼尊卑的礼节不可废弃，那么君臣之间的大义又怎么可以废弃呢？隐居是要想洁身自好，实际却违背了君臣的大义。君子出来做官，并不是贪图富贵功名，为的是要实践君臣的大义；至于良好的政治主张当今行不通，我们也是早就知道的。”

隐士就是隐居不仕之士，即有才能，有学问，能够做官而不去做官也不作此努力的人。他们是道家的前身，这些人对现实的社会政治不降其志，不辱其身，思想上不认输，政治上不合作，认为所有的努力既无济于事，又充满危险。相比之下，孔子的态度就比较积极，尽管处处碰壁，却不改初衷。他的看法是，人如果为了维生而隐居于山林，那与鸟兽就没有什么区别了。

WHY DIDN'T CONFUCIUS TURN RECLUSE?

There used to be two hermits in the State of Chu, Chang Ju and Jie Ni. They lived in seclusion to stay away from the dark society. When Confucius was to leave Chu for the State of Chen via the State of Cai, he happened to pass by two farmers plowing together. They were Chang Ju and Jie Ni. Confucius and his followers could not find the ferry, and sent Zi Lu to ask the two farmers.

Chang Ju asked in reply, "Who is it that holds the rein?"

"Confucius," Zi Lu told him.

"The Confucius from the State of Lu?" Chang Ju went on.

"Yes, he." Zi Lu said.

Chang Ju then said, "He is one that travels through the states. He should know where the ferry is."

Seeing Chang Ju reluctant to answer, Zi Lu turned to Jie Ni. Jie Ni still asked in reply, "Who are you?"

"I am Zhong You." Zi Lu told him.

"So you are Confucius' disciple from Lu?" Jie Ni went on.

"Exactly!" Answered Zi Lu.

Upon that, Jie Ni continued, "It's such a chaotic world, just like the flood sweeping everywhere under Heaven. Such is the world and who can change it? See Confucius, he can never find a place to have his propositions agreed and flees from this man and that. For you would it not be better to follow the one who shuns the world and live a free quiet life, instead of the one who shuns the people." With that Jie Ni went on covering the seeds with soil, and did not show the ferry.

Zi Lu left and reported to Confucius.

Upset with a pause, Confucius sighed, "One cannot associate with birds and beasts. Am I not a member of this human race? Who, then, is there for me to associate with? Were the land under Heaven in peace now, I would not have to run around to initiate reforms."

Confucius himself refused to withdraw from the world, and encouraged the hermits to shoulder up duties for the society as himself. Zi Lu once fell behind while on a journey with Confucius. He chanced upon an old man carrying a basket slung over his staff. Zi Lu walked up asking, "Did you see my Master?" The old man said, "You who with your four limbs do not toil, who do not sift the five grains. Who is your Master?" And with that he planted his staff in the ground and began weeding, while Zi Lu stood by with his hands pressed together. Seeing Zi Lu with good manners, the old man kept Zi Lu for the night, killed a chicken, prepared a dish of millet and introduced him to his two sons. Next day Zi Lu went on his way and reported what had happened to Confucius. Confucius said, "He is a recluse," and told Zi Lu to go back and visit him again.

But on arriving at the place Zi Lu found that the old man had gone out. Thus he passed on Confucius' message to the old man's family, "One who fails to serve his state is to desert the duties one has to the lords. Yesterday he let his two sons out for his observation of the etiquette between the young and the old. If the duties of the young and the old cannot be abolished, how is it that the duties of the lords and subjects were abandoned? Though remaining recluse was a way to keep his integrity, he has in fact gone against the duties of subjects to lords. A gentleman who takes public office aims not fame, but to carry out his duties. That the good political propositions do not prevail, we know well enough beforehand."

A hermit is one who lives in seclusion and rejects public service. He has the talents and knowledge and is competent for a career, but does not intend to or make a try. Such people were the forefathers of Taoists. They adhered to their ambition and integrity. Ideologically, they would not yield, and politically, they would not cooperate. They held the belief that all efforts would amount to nothing except risking all dangers. Comparatively, Confucius was more positive. Though rebuffed almost everywhere, he persisted in his original views that one would not discriminate from birds or beasts if withdrawing into the woods for the sake of making a living.

16. 拜孔子为师

鲁国大夫孟釐子病得很厉害，快要死了。他告诫他的继承人孟懿子说："孔子是圣人的后代，他的家族原先在宋国，他的六世祖孔父嘉在宋国被杀了，他的五世祖逃到了鲁国。弗父何是孔父嘉的高祖父，而宋国的国君宋愍公是弗父何的父亲。本来弗父何是长子，应该由他继承父亲的君位，可是他让给了弟弟宋厉公。弗父何的曾孙正考父，曾经辅佐过宋戴公、宋武公、宋宣公三朝。他三次接受册命，一次比一次恭敬。在正考父庙的一个鼎上铸有铭文，说'第一次接受册命，曲背行礼；第二次接受册命，弯腰行礼；第三次接受册命，俯身行礼。平时走路顺着墙根走，也就没人敢来侮慢我了。用这个鼎做些面糊稀饭来清俭度日。'他就是如此恭敬有礼。我听说这样的圣人的后代，即使不做国君，也会成为一个显赫的人。孔子如今年纪轻轻就懂得这么多事情，熟悉各种礼仪，他恐怕就会成为显赫通达的人。我活不了多久了，等我死了，你们一定要拜他做老师。”孟釐子去世后，他的儿子孟懿子和南宫敬叔前往孔子那儿拜师学礼。那一年，孔子34岁。

如果孔子不发愤学习，怎能受人如此敬重?他曾经说他自己15岁就立下了要好好学习各种知识和本领的志愿。在他17岁的时候，他母亲去世，他想办法找到了父亲的墓地，把父母合葬后，腰间的麻带还没解除，听说鲁国掌权的季孙氏家要宴请士人，他以为自己好歹也是有些知识的人，又是名士的后代，便穿着孝服兴冲冲地跑去了。结果季氏的家臣阳虎呵斥他：“我们请的是有地位的人，并没你的份。”孔子只好退出。也是经过这次挫折，孔子更加勤奋地学习，提高自己的道德修养和各种才能。他30岁的时候，已经找到了自己人生的立足点，对人对事都有了自己的主意。也因此越来越多的人开始投奔到他门下来做弟子。连孟釐子这样的贵族也把自己的孩子送到孔子门下。

孔子不是生而知之的圣人，他的成就来自于他的勤敏好学。他总是抓住一切学习的机会。他说过“三人行，必有我师”，他提出“不耻下问”，他善于取人之长补己之短；他也绝不会不懂装懂，“知之为知之，不知为不知”，这样才会知道得越来越多。他以自己的努力，赢得了世人的尊敬，这敬义绵延千年不衰。

TO FOLLOW CONFUCIUS

Meng Li, a senior minister in the court of Lu, was dying in serious illness. He warned his son and inheritor Meng Yi, saying “Confucius is an offspring of sage. His ancestors were from the State of Song. Kong Fujia, his sixth-generation ancestor, was killed in Song and thus his fifth-generation ancestor fled to Lu. Kong Fujia’s great-grandfather, Fu Fuhe, was the son of Duke Min of Song. Being the eldest son, Fu Fuhe was set to succeed the throne, but he abdicated it to his younger brother, who became known as Duke Li. The great-grandson of Fu Fuhe, Zheng Kaofu, assisted the governance of three generations of reigns in Song: Duke Dai, Duke Wu and Duke Xuan. For three times he received appointments, and each time he showed increased obedience. The epitaph on a vessel in the temple of Zheng Kaofu reads:

'On receiving my first appointment, I bowed my head. On receiving my second appointment, I hunched my back. On receiving my third appointment, I fell upon my face. I ran and hurried along the wall, and nobody would bully me. Use this vessel to cook thick porridge and thin porridge to live on.'

He is such a submissive and obedient person. I heard that the heir of such a sage would make a glorious name if not a king. Knowledgeable of so much at such young age, Confucius is bound for eminence. My days are in sight. After my death, you must follow Confucius." After the death of Meng Li, his sons Meng Yi and Nangong Jingshu recognized Confucius as their master. By then, Confucius was 34.

If without his devotion to studies, how could Confucius receive such reverence? At the age of 15, Confucius aspired to learn all kinds of knowledge. His mother passed away when he was 17. Confucius managed to find out his father's tomb and buried his mother together. When Confucius was still observing mourning with his hemp waistband on, he learned the powerful Ji and Sun clans in the State of Lu were to entertain noted scholars. Thinking himself a scholar in nature and an heir of royal house, Confucius went to the banquet in his mourning dress only to be scolded severely by the Ji's retainer Yang Hu, "We entertain anyone with a status but you!" Confucius had but to withdraw, and that experience spurred him to study even harder to enhance his moral virtues and various skills. At the age of 30, he had already formed his views on things and people, and secured his foothold for life. As a result, more and more came to him as his disciples, including those from noble families like the sons of Meng Li.

Confucius was not born a sage of great learning, but his achievements came from his diligence. He would seize every opportunity to learn, or as he said, "In a group of three, there is always something I can learn from." He was good at learning from other's strong points to make up his own deficiencies, or as he said, "Never feel ashamed to learn from one's subordinates." Confucius would not make a pretence of understanding, or as he said, one would accumulate more and more knowledge if he can "acknowledge what is known as known and what is unknown as unknown." With his untiring efforts, Confucius gained universal reverence, and had cast an influence that never declined through the history.

17. 拜会老子

孟釐子的儿子南宫敬叔拜孔子为师后，有一次跟鲁国国君鲁昭公说："请让我和老师孔子一起前往周的京城洛邑。"鲁昭公就给了他一辆车、两匹马，还有一个仆人一同前往洛邑咨询周礼。周朝的京城洛邑历史悠久，有着丰富的文化宝藏，而且大思想家老子就在那里担任藏书室的管理工作。

老子比孔子年长很多，经验阅历自然也比孔子丰富得多。他担任周朝藏书室的管理工作，接触到的文物史料也就远比孔子广博得多。孔子因此很高兴地拜会了老子，向老子请教了很多东西。老子博学多才，孔子虚心求知，彼此都留下了深刻的印象。等孔子要走的时候，双方都依依不舍了。临别，老子跟孔子说："我听说，富贵人家用财物来给人送行，仁义之人用言语来给人送行。我不是有财有势的人，只好冒充一下仁义的人，送几句话给你。你常说的那些东西，都是古人留下的，他们已经死了，连骨头都烂了，只留下这些话，你不能死抱着。作为一个君子，如果碰上好时候，就坐上车子去做官，如果遇不到好时候，不如像蓬草一样随风转移。我还听说，会做生意的人都把货物囤藏起来，不让外人知道，就像没货似的；具有高尚品德的君子都显得谦恭朴实，看起来傻乎乎的。你应该去掉骄傲，去掉贪欲，去掉做作的姿态，去掉不切实际的妄想，这些对你都没有好处。聪慧明白洞察一切就会惹来杀身之祸，因为那样会喜欢议论别人的长短；博闻善辩宽广弘大也会招来危险，因为那样会抨击别人的丑恶。做别人儿子的时候就不要记得自己，做别人的臣子的时候也不要记得自己，这些时候都不如忘记自身。”

老子的这些话孔子反复咀嚼。回到鲁国后，孔子在自己的弟子面前赞美老子，觉得老子就像传说中的龙一样无法捉摸。“鸟会飞，可还是会被人射下来；鱼会游，可还是会被人钓上来；兽会跑，可还是会落网被捕捉；只有龙，云里来风里去，没有人能控制它。老子就像一条龙。”

老子的临别赠言给了孔子很多启发。他能够更加冷静客观地看待自己及世人世事，在学问上勤勉有加。钦敬他的人越来越多，慕名而来求教的弟子也越来越多。

CALLING ON LAOZI

After Nangong Jingshu, son of Meng Li, followed Confucius, he once requested Duke Zhao of Lu, “Would you please kindly allow my master and I to visit Luoyi, the capital of Zhou?” Duke Zhao agreed and granted a carriage, two horses and a servant to them to learn the rites in Zhou. The capital city of Luoyi had a long history with abundant cultural treasures, where the great thinker,

Laozi, was in charge of the library.

Laozi was much older than Confucius, so naturally he was more knowledgeable. The work in the library provided him more access to the historical and cultural documents. Confucius was thus delighted to call on Laozi with many questions. The two impressed each other tremendously, one for his knowledge and the other for his modesty. By the time Confucius had to leave, they already felt too reluctant to part.

Upon parting, Laozi said, "I hear that the rich present gifts when they part with friends, while the benevolent send words. I am not rich, so I feign myself as the benevolent and give you my words. What you often have on mouth come from the ancients, whose bones might have rotted. You cannot apply them mechanically. When the chance comes, a gentleman goes for an official career. When such a time does not come, one would better follow the wind as a grass. I also hear that a good businessman stores his goods so that he makes believe there is nothing in stock. One with true virtues is modest and humble, and looks silly. You should eliminate your pride, greed, pretence and unreality as they are nothing good for you. If you are clever and insightful, you risk the danger of being killed — because you tend to comment on others' merits and shortcomings. Knowledge, eloquence and generosity may incur similar dangers — because you might be inclined to blame people for their evilness. Do not think of yourself when you are the son or the minister — the best policy under such circumstances is to forget yourself."

The words of Laozi having revolved in his mind, Confucius sang high praises to Laozi to his disciples after returning to Lu. He regarded Laozi as the legendary dragon that was unfathomable, saying, "Birds can fly, but get shot. Fish can swim, but get caught on hooks. Beasts can run, but fall into traps. A dragon, however, can move freely and is beyond the control of anybody. Laozi is just like the dragon."

The parting words from Laozi greatly enlightened Confucius. He took a calmer and more objective attitude toward himself, people and the society. In studies he became more diligent. As a result, he acquired even wider respect and more disciples.

18. 知其不可而为之

孔子在卫国的时候，有一天正在敲着磬消遣，一个背着草筐的人从孔子门前走过，听到磬声，赞叹着说："很有忧世之心啊，这敲磬的人！"听了一会儿，他又说："这个人的想法真是不高明啊！从铿锵坚定的磬声里听得出来，这是个固执而不自量力的人。既然没有人了解自己，就停止算了。《诗经》上说'水深的地方，就穿着衣服游过去；水浅的地方，只要撩起衣服就可以轻松过去。'在这世上为人处世也一样啊，要适合时宜啊。"孔子听了这话，叹了叹气，说："他真是个能够忘却世事的人。人要是都这样处世的话，也就没什么难的了。"

说孔子知其不可为而偏为之远不是一个人的看法。孔子的学生子路在石门外住了一宿，第二天清早就急着赶路。负责开关城门的守门人就问他："你是从哪儿来的？"子路说："我是从孔家来的。"那个守门人就说："就是明明知道无法做还要去做的那个人吗？"

美国女作家赛珍珠说孔子就像耶稣一样，也是“四处周游，他在每一个地方寻找他的追随者。他是贫穷的，受到傲慢者和得势者的拦截、嘲笑，但他不屈不挠，绝不改变他的信念。”多少年来，孔子领着弟子周游列国，四处碰壁，历尽磨难，连子路都说“道之不行，已知之矣”。而孔子却不改初衷，他以强烈的社会责任感表示，如果天下有道，我孔丘自然也就不必来从事这样的改革了。正因为世事不可为，才需要有人来扭转乾坤，澄清天下。

其实，无论是经天纬地的大业，还是日常生活中尴尬生存境遇的处理，只要你不愿向邪恶投降，不愿向愚昧低头，都少不了这“知其不可而为之”的勇气。

TO DO WHAT CANNOT BE DONE

One day when he was in the State of Wei, Confucius was playing the *Qing*, a musical instrument to pass the time. A man carrying a grass basket passed by his door, and admired, “How concerned the player is about the society!” After listening for a while, the man continued, “This is not a wise man! From the sonorous and firm sound of the *Qing* I can tell the man has overrated his abilities. He might just as well stop there if finding no one to understand him. In *The Book of Odes* it reads, ‘If the water is deep, swim across, fully dressed. If the water is shallow, lift up the hem and cross.’ It is the same when one deals with others — to fit his time.” At this, Confucius sighed, “He is a person who easily forgets about the worries. If all are like him, there would be no problems in this world.”

Actually, there had been more than one that thought Confucius was doing what could not be achieved. His disciple Zi Lu once stayed for a night at the Stone Gate. Early the next morning, Zi Lu hurried on for his journey. The gatekeeper asked him, “Where are you from?” “I am from the Kong (Con) family,” answered Zi Lu. “So you mean the Kong,” the gatekeeper asked, “that goes for something cannot be done?”

Pearl S. Buck, an American female writer, remarked that Confucius was just like Jesus Christ, who also “traveled around and looked for his followers everywhere. He is poor. He is blocked and mocked by the arrogant and the powerful. But he never yields or alters his faith.” For years, Confucius led his disciples and travelled through the states, getting snubbed everywhere. Zi Lu even said, “It is little wonder why the Way cannot prevail.” Confucius, however, never changed his mind. With his keen sense of duties for the society, Confucius argued that he would not have to initiate reforms if the Way had existed under Heaven. That things were hard to accomplish made it crucial for some to reform and purify the world.

Actually, be it a grand cause or daily trifles, we need the courage to “do what cannot be done” when we are not willing to succumb to wickedness or ignorance.

19. 要不要先修学识

在鲁定公十二年的时候，子路做了季氏的家臣。然后他就想提携自己的同学、朋友，准备让子羔做费这个地方的首领。子羔差不多比孔子小三四十岁，那时候还很年轻，学问修养也还很不成熟。孔子因此反对子路的提议，说："你这样会害了人家的孩子。"子路却大大咧咧地说，"费这个地方有需要统治管理的人民、官吏，还有需要祭祀的土地神、五谷神的神庙。何必一定要读了书才算是学问呢？"孔子恼火了，"你这样说话来为自己辩解，所以我厌恶像你这样强辩的人。"

孔子是提倡学以致用，并不把书本知识作为主要的或者唯一的学习内容。那他为什么又不赞成子路的提议呢？在《论语·公冶长篇》说到孔子想让漆雕开出任官职，漆雕开表示自己的学识修养还不充分，对自己担任官职没有信心，所以他婉言拒绝了。孔子对漆雕开这样的态度感到非常欣慰，自然也就对子路的强辩感到厌恶了。如果学问修养没有达到一定的程度，怎能胜任治人、安民的工作呢？

当然孔子讲的知识是关于礼乐的知识，并不具有现代知识的内涵。西周时期，人们因社会地位和居住地的不同，就有了贵族、平民和乡野之人的区分。孔子认为， 如果要先用人才，应该选用先学习礼乐的人。因为那些先当官即原来就有爵禄的人，在为官以前，没有接受礼乐知识的系统教育，还不知道怎样为官，便当上了官。这样的人是不可选用的。而那些本来没有爵禄的平民，他们在当官以前已经全面系统地学习了礼乐知识，然后就知道怎样为官，怎样当一个好官。应该说，中国古代知识观重道德、轻科学与孔子的这种看法是一脉相承的。

SHOULD SCHOLARSHIP COME FIRST?

In the 12th year of Duke Ding of Lu, Zi Lu became a retainer in the Ji clan. He then intended to promote his fellow buddies, and thought to name Zi Gao the chief of Fei. Some 30 to 40 years junior to Confucius, Zi Gao was rather young and not yet attained in his scholarship. Thus Confucius opposed the proposal, saying, "You are going to harm such a boy!" Not taking it seriously, Zi Lu said, "What he will take charge of at Fei will be the peasants, officials, and the Holy Ground and Millet. Scholarship does not necessarily come from books." Confucius became angry, "It is remarks of that kind that make me hate glib people."

Confucius did advocate that one should make use of what he had learned and that books were not the sole source of knowledge. Then why did he disagree with Zi Lu? In *The Analects*, Confucius asked one of his disciples Qidiao Kai to take an office, but Qidiao Kai declined as he did not have faith for his scholarship. Confucius was quite delighted with Qidiao Kai. Therefore he felt rather angry toward Zi Lu. Without sufficient scholarly attainment, how could one be qualified in governance and bringing peace to his people?

The knowledge in Confucius' eyes is the one of rites, not the one we define today. During the Western Zhou period, the whole society was divided into nobles, the ordinary and rough countryside people according to social status and residence. Confucius believed that offices should first be given to those who had practiced rites. Those who inherited their official titles were generally not well educated with rites. They became officials before they acquired the understanding of how to be an official. Such people should not be appointed. On the contrary, the ordinary people who had nothing of a title to inherit would have learned systemically the rites before entering the officialdom. Therefore, they understood how to be an official and a good official. Obviously, Confucius' proposition had been on the same track of emphasizing moral virtues while neglecting science in ancient China.

20. 子帅以正，孰敢不正

季康子是鲁哀公时的正卿，是鲁国掌实权的人物。孔子周游列国十四年后返回鲁国，有部分原因就是因为季康子曾受父亲季桓子叮嘱："如果你要辅佐鲁国国君，一定要召回孔子。"孔子是回来了，可孔子对季康子在政治上的僭礼欺君非常不满。季康子问孔子什么是政事，孔子就借机发挥："政就是正，在政位的官员首先自己要正。如果你带头端正自己，谁还敢不正呢？正人必先正己。要求别人做的，首先自己做到；禁止别人做的，自己坚决不做。只有这样才能真正地发挥出一个首领的影响力。"

在《论语》里，我们还能读到类似的话，"其身正，不令而行；其身不正，虽令不从。""苟正其身矣，于从政乎何有？不能正其身，如正人何？"孟子也说"君正莫不正"，从古到今，没有"己不正而能正人者"，自己做不好，怎能要求部下做好？"上梁不正下梁歪"，这是中国百姓普遍认同的观念。教师要求学生的时候，老板要求员工的时候，官员要求百姓的时候，都需要想一想这句话，衡量一下自己的所言所行是否已经可以作为榜样。

日本丰田公司创始人丰田佐吉、丰田喜一郎等人都喜欢读《论语》，丰田喜一郎将“其身正，不令而行”作为座右铭；中国著名企业家柳传志先生，也一直把“其身正，不令而行”这句话放在办公桌上，勉励自己。

TO GOVERN WITH UPRIGHTNESS

Ji Kang was a senior minister and the most powerful in the court of Duke Ai of the State of Lu. After travelling around for 14 years, Confucius returned to Lu partially for the invitation from Ji Kang. His father Ji Huan once warned him, saying, “Should you assist the duke of Lu, you must get Confucius back.” Confucius did come back, but was rather dissatisfied with Ji Kang for overstepping the rites and deceiving the duke. When Ji Kang inquired Confucius on governance, Confucius seized the chance to promote his propositions: “To govern is to be upright. For those who are in power, they need to remain upright in the first place. If they make it, then who else would not? Make oneself upright first before requiring others to be upright. Do something first before requiring others to do the same. Firmly stay away from something before prohibiting others to do it. Only in this way could a ruler exert true influence.”

Similar expressions recurred in *The Analects*: “If one is upright and sets a good example, others will take action without his instructions. If one is not upright or does not set a good example, others will not take action even if he passes down instructions.” “If a man is upright himself, what difficulty will there be for him in public office? If a man cannot be upright, what right does he have in correcting others?" Mencius also said, "If the king is upright, all will be upright." From ancient times onward, "nobody could convince others if he himself is not upright". If you yourself cannot do it well, how can you order the subordinates to meet your requirements? It is universally acknowledged in China that "when those above behave unworthily, those below will follow." This should be a warning sign for the teachers who make requirements on the students, for the bosses on the employees, and for the officials on the ordinary people — we should always examine our own conduct to see if we have made ourselves fair examples.

Sakichi Toyoda and Kiichiro Toyoda, founders of the Japanese Toyota Corp., also loved reading *The Analects*. Kiichiro Toyoda's motto was "If one is upright and sets a good example, others will take action without his instructions." The famed Chinese entrepreneur Liu Chuanzhi also set the same quotation on his table as his reminder.

21. 怎样才是真孝

曾经有很多人问孔子什么是孝。

有一次，樊迟驾车，孔子坐在后面，车子走着，话聊着。孔子告诉樊迟："孟懿子问我什么是孝，我回答他说，孝就是不要违背礼节。"樊迟问老师为什么这么说。孔子说："父母活着的时候，子女要按照礼节侍奉；父母去世，子女要按照礼节安葬，按照礼节祭祀。"

孟懿子的儿子孟武伯也向孔子请教孝道，孔子告诉他："做父母的唯独担忧孩子的身体健康，担忧孩子生病。"孔子的话里隐含着另一层意思，"身体发肤，受之父母，孝之始也"，孩子是父母生命的延续，如果对自己身体不爱护，可以说是对父母心理的伤害。

子游也向老师请教孝道，孔子的回答又不同了，他说："现在所说的孝子，说是能够养活父母就可以了。那人们也在家里养狗养马，如果对父母缺少恭敬之心，那和养狗养马又有什么区别呢？"

还有一个学生子夏也请教过孝的问题。老师是这么说的："孩子在父母面前总是保持颜容的愉悦是很不容易的。长辈有事情，小辈可以替代他们来做，有好吃好喝的先让父兄享用，这样做就能算是孝吗？"孔子的言下之意是"最难的，是一贯用和颜悦色的态度去侍奉父母"。孔子说的一点不假，"久病床前无孝子"，有多少人能一直和颜悦色地对待久卧病床的父母？

除了回答学生们的这些提问外，孔子还说，"父母健在的时候，不要出远门，如果出门，一定要让父母知道是去什么地方。"孔子还说，"做子女的，应该知道父母的年龄，一方面是可以因为父母获得高寿而欢喜，另一方面又该因为父母一年比一年衰老而感到恐惧。"

按照周礼，父母去世后，子女应该守丧三年。大白天睡觉、遭老师责骂的宰予在这个问题上同老师有过讨论。宰予认为守三年的丧，时间太长了。在守丧期间，君子三年不习礼仪，那么礼仪一定生疏了；三年不奏音乐，音乐也会荒废。陈谷子吃完了，新谷子也已经收进仓里，钻燧取火的木头已经按照四季的变化都轮流了一遍，所以守丧一年也就可以了。孔子当时反问他："父母离世一年就吃稻米饭，穿漂亮的锦衣，你觉得心安吗？"宰予倒也坦诚，他说心安。老师也不强求，"既然你觉得心安，你就那样去做好了。君子守丧的时候，吃好东西也不觉得甘美，听音乐不觉得快乐，住在家里也不觉得舒适。现在你觉得安心，那就去做吧。"宰予走了，老师还觉得没把话说透："宰予真是不仁啊，儿女生下来要三年以后才能脱离父母的怀抱，替父母守三年的丧，是天下通行的丧礼啊。宰予呀，他对父母有三年的爱心吗？"因为宰予不愿守丧三年，要减为一年，孔子痛心疾首。父母对孩子的爱毫无保留，而孩子对父母的爱常常是不圆满，不丰厚，不纯粹。

孝是中国古代子女善待父母长辈这一道德行为的表现，根据《说文解字》的解释，"孝，善事父母者"，赡养父母成了中国古人对孝的基本认识。但是孔子不赞成这种观点，他对孝赋予崇敬父母的意义。《礼记》中就汲取了这一思想，说孝有三个层面：首先是尊亲，即崇敬和爱戴父母，立身行道，以扬名显亲，传宗接代；其次是不辱，不亏身体，不辱自身，为亲复仇；最低层面的是养亲，乐其身，顺其意，重其丧。后来的孟子说“不孝有三，无后为大”，也突出了这个意思。正因为这样，孔子对行孝的规定很具体，例如，他说：“守丧的时候，身上长了脓疮就要洗澡，头上长了疖子就要洗头，病了就要喝点酒吃点肉补养一下。不节制哀伤而使身体极度瘦弱，形容枯槁，君子不能那么做。不节制哀伤而送了性命，君子认为这是使父母绝后的不孝行为。”

WHAT IS TRUE FILIAL PIETY?

Many had inquired Confucius on true filial piety.

Once, when Fan Chi was piloting the carriage, Confucius was sitting behind and chatted with him. Confucius told Fan Chi, “Meng Yi once asked me about filial piety and I said: Do nothing against the rites.”

Fan Chi asked his master what he meant. Confucius said, “While one’s parents are alive, one should serve them according to the rites. When they die, one should never fail to comply with the rites of burying and offering sacrifices.”

Meng Wubo, a son of Meng Yi also consulted Confucius on filial piety. Confucius told him, “The parents’ sole concern for their children is their health. They wish their children would never fall ill.” By that Confucius meant to say, “One’s body and hair are given by his parents, which are the first things one should care if he wants to practice filial conduct.” The children carry forward the family line from their parents. If the child does not take good care of his body, he actually hurts the parents.

Zi You asked the same question. To that, however, Confucius had a different answer, "Currently the general belief for a filial son is to feed his parents. In our homes the dogs and horses are also fed. If without a filial heart for the parents, then how could one differentiate from the dogs or the horses?"

Still another disciple Zi Xia asked Confucius the same question. To him, Confucius said, "It is the demeanor that is difficult. The younger ones undertake the hard work when anything has to be done, or serve their elders first with good wine and food. But is it enough to be filial?" By that Confucius meant to say, "The most difficult is to keep pleasant demeanor before parents." How true Confucius had said! As the saying goes, "When ill for long in bed, you won't be watched and fed." But how many bedridden parents could be watched and fed amiably?

Besides answering his disciples, Confucius also remarked, "When parents are alive, one should not travel afar. If a journey has to be made, the directions must be told." "Your parents' age should not be ignored. On the one hand, you would feel happy for their longevity; on the other hand, you should feel worried about their old age."

According to the Rites of Zhou, after the death of the parents, the children should mourn for three years. Zai Yu, who was once blamed by his master for napping in the daytime, had a different opinion. He thought it was too long to mourn for three years. In the meantime, a gentleman would feel rusty on rites and music if without practice for that long. When the old grain was exhausted, the new would have been in store. In procuring fire by fiction, we would have gone through all the changes of wood for that purpose. After a complete year, therefore, the mourning might stop.

Confucius asked him in reply, "If you were, after a year, to eat good rice, and wear embroidered clothes, would you feel at ease?" Frankly as he had been, Zai Yu said yes. Then Confucius did not intend to try hard, saying, "If you could feel at ease, do it. But a gentleman, during the whole period of mourning, does not enjoy pleasant food which he may eat, nor derive pleasure from music which he may hear. He also does not feel at ease, if he is comfortably lodged. Therefore he does not do what you propose. But now you feel at ease and may do it."

Then Zai Yu went out. The Master thought he needed to make his remarks clearer, saying, "This shows his want of virtues. It is not till a child is three years old that he is allowed to leave the arms of his parents. And the three years' mourning has been observed everywhere under Heaven. But Zai Yu, does he have the love for his parents for three years?" So wrenching was Confucius for Zai Yu who had proposed to shorten the three years' mourning to one. It has been that the parents love their children without reservations. The children's love for their parents, however, has always been incomplete, insufficient, and impure.

Filial piety had been the expression of the children's care to their parents in ancient China. According to the *Explaining Words and Articles*, "filial piety" means "to treat parents well." Supporting the parents had been the basic understanding of filial piety among the Chinese. Confucius, however, did not favor such a view. He vested respect as a new layer of meaning to "filial piety". Echoing Confucius was *The Book of Rites*, in which filial piety included three layers of meanings: First, to respect the parents, viz., to respect and love the parents, to practice moral virtues and gain a good fame for them, and to carry on the family line; Second, to take care of oneself, viz., not to allow oneself to be insulted and to revenge for the parents; Third, to care the parents, make them happy, follow their instructions, and observe the mourning rituals.

Then came Mencius who proposed that among the three forms of being unfilial to parents the most severe was not having a descendant. For the same reason, Confucius had a strict definition for filial piety. He said, "When in mourning, if you have festers, you must take a bath. If you have boils in your head, you must wash your hair. If you are ill, you should have some drink or meat to nourish your body. A gentleman cannot make his appearance withered and yellow or become skinny and weak because of grief. If one loses his life for grief, a gentleman takes it as violating filial piety because he had cut off the family line."

22. 干大事还是干小事

有一天，子路、曾皙、冉有、公西华四位弟子陪着孔子一起坐着聊天。

孔子说："因为我的年龄比你们大些，你们就不敢把心里话爽快地说出来，不要这样拘束嘛。你们平常总说'别人不知道我。'那现在我们假设有人知道你们，你们准备怎样施展自己的才学呢？"

子路还是一样地率性，不假思索地回答："假如一个拥有一千辆兵车的国家，夹在几个大国之间，常受到他们的侵犯。除了人祸，国内还有天灾，闹饥荒什么的，这样的国家，让我仲由去治理三年，只要三年就够了，可以使全国的人民都有战斗的勇气，还能让人民知晓道义。"

孔子听了，笑了笑。又问："冉求，你怎么样？"冉求回答道："一个方圆六七十里，或者五六十里的国家，要是让我治理，等到三年，就能够让老百姓丰衣足食。至于礼乐，那就要等有才德的君子了。”

孔子转向公西华：“公西赤，你呢？”公西赤这样回答：“不能说我自己能干，可是我愿意学习。比如有宗庙祭祀的工作，或者同别国的盟会，我愿意穿着礼服，戴着礼帽，做个小小的司仪官。”

孔子最后问曾皙：“曾点，你呢？”曾点正在一旁弹着瑟，乐声渐渐稀疏，铿地停了下来。曾点放下瑟站起来，恭恭敬敬地答道：“我和他们三人的志向不一样。”孔子说：“不一样就不一样，这有什么妨碍呢，我们只是在谈各人的志向呀。说说吧。”曾皙就说了：“暮春三月的时候，做好春服，约了五六个成年人，带着六七个孩子，沐浴在沂水河里，之后坐在舞雩台上享受清风，然后唱着歌，走上回家的路。”孔子听了，叹息着，脸上甚至露出神往的样子，“我赞成曾点的想法啊！”子路、冉有、公西华都走了，曾皙落在后面，他还有问题。看三位同学都走远了，曾皙问老师：“他们三人所谈的想法怎样？”孔子淡淡地回答：“也就是每个人谈谈自己的志向罢了。”曾皙紧追着问：“那您为什么要笑仲由？”老师便解释了刚才听子路说完后为什么笑：“治理一个国家要依靠礼，仲由说话不谦虚，所以笑他。”曾皙还是不满足，“那冉求说的就不是治理国家吗？”“怎么能说方圆六七十里或者五六十里就不是治理国家呢？”“那么公西赤说的就不是治理国家吗？”“宗庙祭祀，诸侯盟会，这些难道不是诸侯治理国家的事情吗？要是公西赤只能干小事，那么谁能干大事呢？”

弟子们在老师的鼓励下畅所欲言，交流各人的志向。老师并未一一点评，给子路的是一个“笑脸”，只有对最后曾皙所说的是频频点头，明确地说出了自己的看法。事后在曾皙的不断追问下，老师才说了原因。子路一直是个好勇仗义的猛士，当他用那样铿锵有力的语言表达他能治理一个国家的信心时，讲究谦逊好礼的老师忍不住要笑他。而像公西赤、曾皙那样，虚怀若谷，深得老师思想精髓的熏陶，表明自己只能做点微小的事情，甚合老师心意。一个真有雄才大略的人，他会不动声色，不露锋芒，只有在目标出现的时候，他才会动如脱兔，以敏捷的才思、坚定的意志、周密的谋略去赢得目标。

“一屋不扫何以扫天下”，从孔子时代起，中国人就提倡凡事从小处着手，一个人切不可好高骛远，不可眼高手低，诸如此类。千年来中国人讲究谦谦方是君子，尤其在师长面前，如果锋芒毕露，那必定会被视为“初生牛犊”，没有心计，缺乏城府，基本上属于“有勇无谋”类的。不过，随着西风东渐，随着时代的发展，如果今天这子路、冉有、公西华、曾皙分别到公司去应聘，尤其是到跨国大公司，面试官是否会像孔子一样笑子路而赞曾皙，已经很难说了。

INTENT ON A GRAND CAUSE OR LITTLE AFFAIRS?

One day, Confucius was chatting with his four disciples: Zi Lu, Zeng Xi, Ran You and Gongxi Hua.

Confucius said, “Do not feel constrained simply because I am a senior. You always complain ‘others do not recognize my merits.’ Now suppose someone does recognize your merits, how are you going to display your learning and talents?”

Straightforward as he had been, Zi Lu replied promptly, “Were I to govern a state with a thousand chariots, hemmed in by powerful neighbors, or even invaded by hostile armies, with disasters and famine to boot, I would resume the people’s morale and sense of virtues within a matter of three years.”

Smiling, Confucius turned to Ran You, saying, “What about you?” Ran You replied, “Were I to govern a state that covers sixty or seventy square *li* or say fifty to sixty square *li*, I could bring it about that the common people should lack for nothing within a matter of three years. But as to rites and music, I should have to leave them to a real gentleman.”

Then Confucius turned to Gongxi Hua, "And you, Gongxi Hua?" Gongxi Hua said, "I do not say I could do this; but I should like at any rate to be trained for it. In ceremonies at the ancestral temple or interstate summit, I would like, clad in the ceremonial gown and cap, to play the part of junior assistant."

Finally, Confucius asked Zeng Xi, "Now, Zeng Xi, what about you?"

The notes of the zither he was softly fingering died away; he put it down, rose and replied, saying, "I fear that I differ from the other three in my choice."

Confucius said, "What harm is there in that? All that matters is that each should name his desire."

Zeng Xi then said, "In late spring, when the spring clothes are made, to go with five or six adults and six or seven kids, we bath in River Yi, take the air at the Rain Dance altar, and then go home singing."

Heaving a deep sigh, Confucius seemed to be charmed, "I am with Zeng Xi!"

When the three others left, Zeng Xi stayed behind and asked, "What do you think of their choices?"

Casually, Confucius said, "We were merely talking about personal desires."

Zeng Xi went on, "Then why did you smile at Zi Lu?"

Confucius explained, "It is upon the rites that the governance of a state depends, but his words lack modesty. That is why I smiled at him."

Zeng Xi was not satisfied and went on asking, "Was Ran You talking about the governance of a state?" "Could a domain of sixty or seventy square *li* or fifty to sixty square *li* not be a state?" "Wasn't Gongxi Hua talking about the governance of a state?" "Aren't the ceremonial occasions in the ancestral temple and diplomatic gatherings not matters which concern rulers of feudal states? If Gongxi Hua plays only a minor part, who could play the major role?"

His disciples were encouraged to speak out their desires freely, and the Master did not comment everyone except a "smiling face" to Zi Lu, and finally nodding his agreement at Zeng Xi. It was because Zeng Xi's insistence that Confucius gave his explanations. Zi Lu was known for his chivalrous valor.

Thus when he expressed his confidence in governing a state with his powerful words, his Master who always emphasized modesty and rites would laugh at him. While for the modest ones like Gongxi Hua and Zeng Xi that had grasped the essence of their Master's thoughts, Confucius felt readily pleased to hear their commitment to little affairs. One with real talents and bold vision would not show it out until the right chance comes when he would seize fast. Until then, he would strive for his goal with his wits, perseverance and strategies.

"If you do not begin by sweeping your room, how can you sweep to victory across the world?" From Confucius' time, the Chinese people have long emphasized the significance to begin with little affairs. One should not aim too high while taking no solid steps. Throughout the millennium, the Chinese have long regarded those "modest" as being "gentlemen". If someone failed to restrain his talents, especially before the seniors and teachers, he would be regarded as a "new-born calf" lacking calculation or depth — that would surely be labeled with "foolhardy". However, we are now in a time of fast social progress, coupled with the western culture spreading into the east. Should Zi Lu, Ran You, Gongxi Hua, and Zeng Xi stand for interviews in especially multinational corporations, it would be hard to tell whether the judges would still smile at Zi Lu and praise Zeng Xi.

23. 如何判断一个人的好坏

子贡问老师：“如果乡里的人都喜欢他，这个人怎么样？”老师挺干脆地回答：“没法肯定。”子贡又问：“那如果乡里的人都厌恶他，这个人怎么样？”老师回答说：“也还是不能肯定。不如乡里的善人都喜欢他，乡里的恶人都厌恶他。”

让一个人来判断另一个人是好是坏，从来都不是一件容易的事。倘若把这个人放在一个群体中，以众人雪亮的眼睛来进行观察，以众人智慧的心灵来感受，这个人基本上就无处遁逃了，是好是坏，可以听众人的意见来判定。但是，众人之口也难免会产生“铄金”一类的后果。所以，孔子教导我们，要把众人分成两类，善类和恶类，截然相反的这两类人对同一个人的看法可以对照可以互补，倘若善人都喜欢而恰巧恶人都厌恶，那这个人的好坏基本上可以把握了。

不过，孔子还教导我们，除了听众人的意见外，不妨再结合自己的亲自观察。深入细微的观察，更可以使我们获得一份亲身的体验与独到的见解。“大家都厌恶的人，我一定要仔细观察；大家都喜欢的人，我也一定要仔细观察！”孔子自己就是这样做的——不独断，也不盲信。是啊，万一碰到一群“乡愿”（孔子眼里那些谁也不得罪的好好先生）——对什么人都一味讨好，他们的意见对你的判断毫无作用。

乡里众口一词的好人“乡愿”，也不是真的好；相反，孔子认为这样的乡愿，是“德之贼”——此类表面忠厚而内心奸诈的伪君子，其实是戕害道德的蟊贼。

HOW TO JUDGE A PERSON?

Zi Gong asked the Master, “If one is favored by all the people, how about this man?” The Master answered without hesitation, “It is not enough.” Zi Gong went on, “If one is hated by all the people, how is he?” Confucius said, “It is not enough either. It’s easier to judge a person who is loved by the good and hated by the wicked.”

It is never easy to judge whether someone is good or bad. If we put him into a group and let the public watch and judge, he would be seen clearly. But the “many mouths” of the public might also show negative impact as to “melt the true metal”. Thus Confucius told us we should put people into two groups, the good and the wicked. The opinions of the two diametrically opposite groups of people may complement each other. That could serve for our cross reference. If one is favored by all the good and hated by the whole bad lot, it would become rather easy for us to make our judgment.

However, Confucius also instructed that we should observe with our own eyes besides referring to the public opinion. As such, we would gain a personal experience and an insight. To quote Confucius, "I would observe carefully the one that is hated by all. I would also observe carefully the one that is loved by all." The Master practiced what he had advocated: not to dogmatize, nor to follow blindly. How true that was! When one meets a bunch of hypocrites (Mr. Good Well in Confucius' term), he would be able to make no reference to their opinions at all.

Surely, such a Mr. Good Well would not do real good. As a matter of fact, Confucius regarded such "hypocrites of virtue", courteous outside but deceitful inside, as harmful moral pests.

24. 雪中送炭与锦上添花

擅长外交的公西华出使去了齐国，家中无人照料。他的同学冉有去孔子那儿替公西华的母亲要粟米。孔子说："给她一釜（釜是当时的量器，每釜的容量是六斗四升，大致相当于现在的20公斤）吧。"冉有请求再增加一点，孔子就说："那就给她一庾（庾也是当时的量器，容量差不多是16斗，大致相当于现在的50公斤）吧。"结果冉有一给给了五秉（秉也是当时的容器，据说容量差不多是160斗，大致相当于现在的500公斤）。孔子知道后认为冉有大可不必，说："公西赤出使到齐国，有壮硕的马拉着车，有又轻又暖的裘皮衣服穿在身。我听到这样的一种说法：君子应该周济穷人的急难，但不需要增加富人的财富。"

还有两件事可以更深刻地理解孔子对冉有 "不该给却给" 的批评。事情一：孔子在鲁国做司寇的时候，请学生原思做了自己的管家，俸禄是900斗谷子。原思觉得太多了，推辞不肯接受。孔子说："没关系，不要推辞了，如果你觉得多余，就给你的乡亲们吧。”原思家非常贫穷，孔子特意多给俸禄，以便改善他一家的生活，如果有多余，还可以救济原思的乡亲们。原思的推辞变成了“该取却不取”，孔子也对他进行了教育。

事情二：冉有是孔子的学生。有一天，孔子对他的其他弟子们说：“你们把冉有轰出去，他不再是我的学生了。”为什么？因为鲁国权臣季氏的家财已经超过了周公，他的家臣冉有却还要帮他苛征赋税，搜刮民财，去增加他的财富。孔子深恶痛绝，号召弟子们群起攻之。

孔子的态度很明确，君子要救人急难，而不必锦上添花。在现实社会中，我们可以看到有权有势什么也不缺的人，偏偏常有人送礼上门；而那些饥寒交迫缺衣少食的人，往往无人问津，即便卧病在床，也无人相助，只能生死由命。如果大家都像孔子一样来矫正俗世不合适的“取和予”，那么社会就会更加和谐而安定。“贫居闹市无人问，富在深山有远亲”，“不信但看筵中酒，杯杯先劝有钱人”的诗句也可以重写了。

SENDING FIREWOOD IN THE WINTER OR GILDING ON THE GOLD?

When Gongxi Hua, who was good at diplomacy, was sent on a diplomatic mission to the State of Qi, he had to leave his family unattended. His fellow disciple Ran You asked for grain allowance on behalf of Gongxi Hua's mother. Confucius said, "Give her one *fu* (a measure of about 20 kilos)." Ran You asked for more, and Confucius said, "Then give her a *yu* (a measure of about 50 kilos)." However, Ran You gave her 5 *bings* (a measure of about 500 kilos). After learning that, Confucius thought that it was unnecessary for Ran You to be that generous, saying, "On his mission to Qi, Gongxi Hua rides a carriage pulled by fine horses and wears light and warm fur clothes. I have heard that a gentleman should help the poor out, but not add to the wealth of the rich."

Two similar cases further exemplified Confucius' criticism on Ran You. The first happened during Confucius tenure as the Minister of Justice in Lu. He had his disciple Yuan Si be his home steward, and the reward was 900 *dous* of grains. Yuan Si regarded that as being too much and would not accept. Confucius told him, "Never mind, but if you feel it's too much you might just as well give the extra to your fellow villagers." As a matter of fact, Confucius knew the family of this disciple lived in poverty, and thus intentionally gave a big allowance to help his family and even his fellow villagers. Yuan Si was declining what he "should" accept. Therefore, he also received a lecture from the Master.

Another happened to his disciple Ran You. One day, Confucius told his disciples, "Turn Ran You out! He is no longer my disciple." Why? The powerful Ji clan in the State of Lu had already surpassed the wealth of Duke Zhou. Ran You as a retainer in the Ji clan still helped collect excessive taxes to add to their wealth. Confucius hated that bitterly and thus called on his disciples to condemn Ran You.

Confucius had clear-cut attitudes. A gentleman should help those in need, but not gild the gold. In our life, we often see those in power receive gifts, but those in need are neglected. People might be bedridden with illness and remain helpless, putting their life into the hands of fate. Should all of us learn from Confucius to rectify the improper "giving and taking", we would be living in a more harmonized and stable society. By then, we would revise sayings like "If you are poor, even if you live in a crowded city you will be alone. But if you are rich, even if you live in uninhabited mountains the most distant relatives will flock to you"; and "Don't you see this at a feast — all the toasts go first to the richest?"

25. 厌恶与喜欢

子贡总能提出一些特别的问题。他问老师："君子也有他所厌恶的人吗？"孔子说："当然有他厌恶的人。厌恶那些到处宣扬别人坏事的人；厌恶那些地位低下却诋毁上级的人；厌恶勇猛却缺乏礼数的人；厌恶勇敢果断却不通事理的人。"孔子说完，反问学生："端木赐啊，你是不是也有厌恶的人啊？"子贡也就不客气地说出来了："我厌恶那些窃取别人的成果而自以为聪明的人；厌恶那些不懂谦逊而自以为勇敢的人；厌恶那些揭别人的隐私而自以为率直的人。"

师徒二人坦率地说出了自己所厌恶的人——或违背义理，或假托义理。这几类人尽管受人厌恶，可至今未曾绝种。诸如喜欢诋毁、不知礼数、不通事理、剽窃他人成果、鲁莽、搬弄是非、长舌妇(夫)等等。我们都不会喜欢这样的人，可为什么这样的人还是朝朝代代都层出不穷呢？如果天天像孔子的学生曾参一样反省自己"为别人做事是否已经尽心尽力？同朋友交往是否诚实而值得人信赖？老师传授的学业是否已经温习”，每天把自己做人做事做学问的状况，都仔细地审视一下，可以少遭人厌。

那么，什么样的人受人喜欢？孔子给过答案：在家里懂得孝敬老人、体谅父母；出门在外，对待朋友们就像自己的兄弟姊妹一般，不势利、不自私；说话谨慎负责，不信口开河，不夸夸其谈；一旦许了诺言，一定会努力兑现，负起责任；心里怀着对世界及世人的爱，热心帮助别人，成全别人；喜欢学习，爱读书，决不庸庸碌碌。这些对“弟子”的朴实的希望，至今还在闪闪发亮。

HATE AND LOVE

Zi Gong always had some special questions. He asked Confucius, “Does a gentleman have someone to hate?”

“Surely,” Confucius said, “He hates those who make known publicly what is hateful in others. He hates those who dwell in low status but revile all who are above them. He hates those who love deeds of daring but neglect rites. He hates those who are active and venturesome, but are violent in temper.”

Turning to his disciple, Confucius asked, “Then what about you? Do you have someone to hate as well?”

Zi Gong answered frankly, “I hate those who mistake cunning for wisdom. I hate those who mistake insubordination for courage. I hate those who mistake tale-bearing for honesty.”

The Master and his disciple talked about the person they hate — those who either violate or make pretense of rites. Disgusting as they have always been, such people still exist. These people have a liking to slander, ignore rites or logic, pirate others' achievements, rush fences, gossip, so on and so forth. None of us like such people, but why they are there through generations? Zeng Shen, one of Confucius' disciples, examined his conducts every day: "Have I been faithful in doing things for others? Have I been trustworthy in contacts with friends? Have I reviewed and practiced what my teacher has taught me?" Should one follow the suit of Zeng Shen, he would not be hated as much.

Then what kind of person is loved? Confucius' has supplied us an answer: one that remains filial and considerate to his parents at home, that is not snobbish or selfish when out with friends and treats them as brethren, that is cautious in talk and never brags, that lives up to his promises, that cherishes a love for people and the world, and that loves reading so as not to be a good-for-nothing.

All the hopes that Confucius had on his disciples still have their worth now.

26. 孔子选婿

孔子生活的时代自然还没有自由恋爱，都是媒妁之言，父母之命。孔子也是身为父亲的人，他要给儿子娶媳妇，给女儿选丈夫。我们不知道他儿子孔鲤娶了谁，但在《论语》中记载了他给女儿选丈夫的片段。

孔子有一个学生叫公冶长，他家境贫寒，靠打柴为生，家里还有一位老母亲。据说他因为自幼在山中生活，与禽兽打交道，因而能够辨别鸟兽鸣叫的意思。有一次，公冶长在山中听到一只乌鸦在叫："公冶长，公冶长，前山有只大绵羊，你吃肉来我吃肠，拿回羊皮做衣裳。"公冶长跟着乌鸦到了前山，果然看到一只死羊，内肠已经被吃完了，他便把羊皮扒下，把羊肉带回家给母亲吃，还想给母亲做件羊皮袄。可没想到刚好被找羊的失主看到，便说是公冶长偷了他的羊，公冶长怎么解释也不顶用，被送到衙门治罪。公冶长没办法，便把乌鸦报信的事情说给审判官听。审判官当然不相信，谁能听懂乌鸦的话啊？这不明显是强词夺理嘛，公冶长便被判入狱。后来审判官在庭审另一宗案件的时候，梁上的燕窝里小燕子们在嬉戏，不小心一只小燕子掉了下去，摔在了公案上。审判官怕影响堂审，就把小燕子放进了抽屉。燕子妈妈见少了一个孩子，就在公堂内乱飞乱叫，冲着审判官撞，赶也赶不走。审判官只好停下堂审，暂时回避了。听着燕子的叫声，突然想起押在牢里的公冶长，审判官想不妨让这个自称懂鸟语的人来听听燕子在“说”什么。公冶长被带到大堂，仔细听了听燕子的叫唤，告诉审判官，“燕子在找她的孩子，老爷您把小燕子给放在抽屉里了。”审判官一听，真是这样，看来公冶长还真的懂鸟语。公冶长因此也被释放了。就是这个坐牢的公冶长成了孔子的女婿。孔子摆脱了门第观念，也不在乎彩礼聘礼，孔子看中的是公冶长的德学兼备。他凭借自己细致的观察，判定公冶长是被冤枉的，说：“可以把女儿嫁给这样的人做妻子。虽然他被关在监狱里，但并不是他的罪过。”

孔子给自己选了女婿。在这之前，他还给哥哥的女儿、即自己的侄女也选了丈夫。孔子的跛脚哥哥比孔子要大很多，侄女也比自己的女儿大。按照周礼的规定，兄不娶，弟不能越婚；姐不嫁，妹不能先配。所以，孔子严格遵照周礼，先选定了侄女婿。这侄女婿也是他自己的学生，叫南宫适。为什么选南宫适，我们看看孔子对他的评论：“当国家政治清明的时候，他总能被朝廷任用而不至被废弃不用；当国家政治黑暗的时候，他总能言行谨慎而不至于受刑罚。”由此可见，南宫适是一个对处世哲学很有修养的人，非常符合孔子说过的“邦有道，危言危行；邦无道，危行言孙”，就是在国家大治的时候，言行都应该正直，在国家昏暗的时候，行为要正直，但言语要谨慎。南宫适无论在治世还是乱世，他的言行都很得当，这样的人怎能不为孔子喜欢？

孔子选婿着重个人的德行，他的标准，我们仍可借鉴。

CONFUCIUS' SELECTING HIS SON-IN-LAW

In Confucius' time, people had no freedom to choose their spouse but to follow the matchmakers and parents. As a father, Confucius also had to find a wife for his son and a husband for his daughter. It is hard for us to find out which lady he chose for his son, but we do find records of his son-in-law in *The Analects*.

A disciple of Confucius, named Gongye Chang, was born in a poor family and lived on cutting woods with his old mother. It was said that because Gongye Chang had lived in the woods since he was a boy, he could understand the sounds of birds and beasts. One day, Gongye Chang heard a crow yelling, "Gongye Chang, Gongye Chang, there is a big sheep in the front mountain. You eat its meat and I eat the intestines. You take the hide back to make dresses." Gongye Chang followed the crow there and did find a dead sheep, whose intestines had been eaten. So Gongye Chang tore down the hide, planning to take the meat home and with the hide to make a warm dress for his mother. However, the owner of the sheep ran across him and accused him of theft. All his explanations useless, Gongye Chang was hauled into the *yamen*. Again, Gongye Chang told the judge his story. But the judge would not believe that he could understand the sounds of a crow. Gongye Chang was regarded to have invented a story. As a result, Gongye Chang was thrown into prison.

Later, when the judge was in court hearing another case, the little swallows were playing in the nest on the beam. Suddenly, a little one fell down onto the judge's table. Fearing it would disturb the case, the judge put it into his drawer. When the mother swallow realized a baby was missing, she cried and swirled in the court and dashed toward the judge. The judge had to adjourn. Hearing the swallows, it occurred to him that the Gongye Chang in the prison had claimed to understand birds. So Gongye Chang was brought in. After hearing carefully for a while, Gongye Chang told the judge, "The swallow is looking for her baby. But you have put it in your drawer." Now the judge had come to realize that Gongye Chang did understand birds, and released him.

It was this Gongye Chang who had been in prison that became Confucius' son-in-law. Confucius paid no heed to family status or betrothal gifts. What Confucius appreciated was that he was a man of learning and virtue. After careful observation, Confucius believed Gongye Chang was wronged, saying, "I might marry my daughter to this man. Though in prison, it was not his fault."

Besides his own son-in-law, Confucius also found husband for his niece, the daughter of his elder brother. His crippled brother was much older than him and the niece was also a senior to his own daughter. According to Zhou rites, the younger brother should not marry before the elder brother and the younger sister should not marry before the elder sister. Confucius strictly followed the rites and thus found for his niece her husband, who was also his disciple named Nangong Shi.

The reason to choose Nangong Shi, to quote Confucius, was, "When the state has the Way, he is not abandoned. When the state does not follow the Way, he is free from punishment and persecution." From this, we could tell Nangong Shi was a man with good cultivation in the philosophy of life, which conformed with what Confucius once remarked: "When the state is running properly, be truthful in your words, and act in proper manner. When the state is in disorder, act in proper manner but be cautious in speech." No matter it was in peace or chaos, Nangong Shi could always keep his conduct and words proper. How could Confucius dislike such a man like this?

We could still learn from Confucius' criteria of emphasizing moral virtues in selecting his son-in-law.

27. 孔子送给鲁定公的两句话

鲁定公和孔子的一次谈话，可以说言不多，意却精。其中最关键的两句话，至今闪闪发光。

鲁定公问："一句话就可以振兴国家，有这样的话吗？"孔子回答："一句话自然不可能期望它有这么大的功效啊！人们常说这样一句话，'做国君难，做臣子也不容易。'从这句话我们知道，假如知道做国君的困难，不就近似于一句话就可以振兴国家了吗？"鲁定公又问："一句话就会葬送国家，有这样的话吗？"孔子回答："一句话自然不可能期望它起这么大的效果啊！人们常说这样一句话，'我做国君没什么快乐，只是因为我说话没人敢违背我啊！'要是国君的话说得对而没有人敢违背，不是很好吗？可要是国君的话说得不对而没人敢违背，不就近似于一句话就可以葬送国家吗？"

我们无法确切地判断这两句话是不是孔子说的，也许真的是社会上流传的，也许是孔子借口“人们”说的话。但确确实实是孔子把这两句话拈来送给鲁定公，并且做了解释。鲁定公要的一言兴邦和一言丧邦，孔子拿不出，不认为一句话的力量有如此之强，足以振兴一个国家或者毁灭一个国家。但社会上流传的这两句话，应该是作为对历史上王朝兴衰的总结流传下来的。国君在一国之内拥有至高无上的权力和地位，但国君并不能只享受权力地位带来的优越，同时也要承担权力地位带来的义务。因此，做国君——当然是好的国君——并不容易。从人的本性来说，随心所欲应该是最快乐的。但如果国君只顾自己的快乐，无休止地满足自己的欲望，刚愎自用，无反省之心，使很多曲意奉承的人对君王的错言错行噤口不提，这时国家的衰亡也就不远了。

孔子送给鲁定公的这两句话，力量不在于言，而在于言外之意——一国之兴与一国之亡，关键在于国君的治国之心。小到一家，大到一国，这治家治国之理如出一辙——用心、倾听。

CONFUCIUS' TWO STATEMENTS FOR DUKE DING OF LU

Confucius and Duke Ding of the State of Lu once had a conversation. Though short, there were two statements showing lasting worth.

Duke Ding asked, “Is there such a thing as a single statement that would bring about prosperity to a state?”

Confucius replied, “A statement itself does not have such effect. People say, ‘It is difficult to be a ruler and not easy to be a minister.’ If one understands the difficulty of being the ruler, doesn't it almost to say that a word can bring prosperity to a state?”

Duke Ding continued asking, "Is there such a thing as a single statement would bring about the loss of a state?"

Confucius replied, "Similarly, a statement itself does not have such effect. People have said, 'There is no happiness greater than being the ruler, for his words would never be resisted.' If what the ruler says is correct, not resisting it would be good. But if what he says is not good but without resistance, then isn't it tantamount to saying a single statement would bring about the loss of a nation?"

We are not sure whether Confucius said these words himself or they were mere hear-and-say. It was, however, true that Confucius presented these words to Duke Ding with his own interpretation. When questioned by Duke Ding, Confucius was caught resourceless but believed there were no such words as would lead directly to the thriving or ruining of a state.

However, these words should have been a summary of the rise and decline of the history. The ruler of a state had the ultimate power and status, but he should not merely indulge in the powers without taking due responsibilities. Therefore, Confucius believed it was not easy to be a ruler, let alone a good one. For the human beings by nature, it meets the ultimate desire for one to do anything at will. However, a state would see quick decline if the ruler cares only about personal enjoyments, endless desires, and remains opinionated without self examination, with many flatterers around but being blind to his ill conducts.

The real significance of Confucius' words to Duke Ding lied not in the words themselves, but in the meaning they carried, viz., the ruler's emphasis for governance held the crucial stake for prosperity and decline. The key to ruling, be it a family or a state, is to show the attention.

28. 孔子也矛盾

鲁国有三家极有实力的贵族，都是原来鲁桓公的后代，称为“三桓”。一家是孟孙氏，就是后来做了孔子学生的孟懿子、南宫敬叔他们（孔子的侄女许配给了南宫敬叔）；一家是叔孙氏，还有一家是季孙氏，其中以季孙氏一家的势力为最大。这时季氏家中的季平子把持国政，鲁昭公尽管很讨厌他，也没有办法对付他。后来季平子和另外一个叫郈昭伯的贵族起了纠纷，郈昭伯向鲁昭公诉冤，鲁昭公便趁机讨伐季平子。可是季平子联合三桓，反而打败了鲁昭公，鲁昭公只能逃到齐国，后来死在齐国，鲁昭公的弟弟继位，就是鲁定公。鲁定公五年，季平子也死了，他的继承人则是季桓子。季氏家族连续几代把持了鲁国的政权，鲁国国君等同于木偶。有意思的是，季桓子尽管还是大权在握，但他也常被自己的一些强势的家臣威胁，就像他自己胁迫鲁定公一样。他的三大家臣，仲梁怀、阳货和公山不狃之间也在明争暗斗，想独揽权益。仲梁怀和阳货发生冲突，公山不狃出面劝解了两方。仲梁怀却更加嚣张，阳货便囚禁了他。季桓子看他们闹得实在不像话，也出面干涉，却根本没被阳货放在眼里，把季桓子也一起囚禁了起来，直到季桓子认输才放了他。这在孔子眼里，无疑是与周礼背道而驰的。所以当阳货为了扩大自己的威望，想要见孔子，请孔子去他家里时，孔子二话不说就拒绝了。

连季氏都能把持的阳货怎会就此善罢甘休。他想出一计，差人给孔子送去一头蒸熟的小猪。按照当时的礼仪，受礼的人得上门拜谢送礼的人，这样阳货算定孔子不得不去他家见他。对孔子而言，面见权臣是逾礼的，受礼不回拜也是逾礼的，那怎么才能两全其美？于是孔子想了一个办法，他选了个特殊的时间，知道阳货不在家的时候，他便去阳货家拜谢。

都说人算不如天算，孔子算好在阳货不在家的时候去回谢是最佳时机，偏偏老天不作美，竟然在半路上碰到了阳货！两人相遇，阳货先开了口，“请过来，我有话对你说。”阳货大概猜出了为何在路上遇见孔子，口气有些不善。“身怀本领而对国家的事情稀里糊涂，可以称得上仁吗？”孔子听出其言下之意，也干脆地回答：“不可以。”阳货又逼近一步，“心里喜欢从政却屡屡失去机会，可以称得上聪明吗？”孔子还是干干脆脆地回答：“不可以。” 阳货见孔子步步后退，自己占了上风，便更直接地说：“日月飞逝，时间不会再回来了。”一直在为恢复周礼殷殷努力的孔子一方面不愿意去做有损周礼的事，一方面又要在这样的乱世中保护自己，因此就顺着阳货的意思说：“好，我打算去做官了。”其实这只是孔子的权宜之计，这个阳货后来在军事上失败了，逃去了齐国，此事也就不了了之。

除了阳货之外，季桓子还有一个叫公山不狃的强势家臣。这个公山不狃也没有吸取仲梁怀和阳货的教训，公元前501年占据了鲁国一个叫费的地方，想利用这个地方来抗衡季桓子。他也来召见孔子，孔子却想前往。学生子路得知后，很不高兴地说：“没地方去就算了，干吗要去公山氏那儿呢？”孔子说：“那召我去的人难道没有用意吗？假如有人用我，我将使一个新的东周王朝重生。”

孔子拒绝了阳货却想靠近公山不狃，孔子的学生自然大为不解。其实还不光是公山不狃，孔子还看好一个叫佛肸的人。佛肸是晋国大夫赵简子的邑宰，占据了中牟这个地方来反叛赵简子。他也召请孔子，孔子也想前往。学生子路又是一番疑问：“从前我曾听您说过‘亲身做坏事的人，君子是不去结交的’，如今佛肸占据中牟，要起兵反叛，您却要去他那儿，这是什么道理啊？”孔子解释了自己的想法：“是的，我以前说过这样的话。不过不是有所谓的坚固吗？真正坚固的东西是磨不薄的；不是有所谓的洁白吗？真正洁白的东西是染不黑的；我总不能做匏瓜一直挂到老，而不能食用。”孔子用比喻说明了自己的立场不会因为身处乱世而受玷污，而且君子不能只是在乱世中守身如玉，独善其身，更要想办法改造这个乱世。“天下有道，丘不与易也”，正因为天下无道，孔子才要去积极参与改造。在他心里，公山、佛肸目前是在叛乱，如果能够改变他们，叛乱将会变成重振周礼的起点。

然而孔子终究还是哪儿也没去，他是矛盾的。在各国诸侯彼此争斗，都想把持天子，诸侯下的卿大夫想把持各自的国君，卿大夫下的家臣亦在争权夺利的大背景下，公山、佛肸是否会如他所想的那样改变？叛乱会否平定？周礼能否从下层开始振兴？孔子也不免有惑。人说孔子不识时务，看来也未必全是。

CONFUCIUS CAUGHT IN DILEMMA

There were three powerful clans in the State of Lu, and all were descendents of Duke Huan and thus were called “*Three Huan*”: Meng Sun clan (including Meng Yizi and Nangong Jingshu who later became Confucius’ disciples; Confucius married his niece to Nangong Jingshu), Shu Sun clan, and Ji Sun clan. The most powerful was the Ji Sun clan, in which Ji Ping held the main power. Though Duke Zhao disliked him, he had no way to handle.

Later, Ji Ping had a dispute with another aristocrat Hou Zhaobo, who then turned to Duke Zhao for justice. Thus Duke Zhao took the advantage and launched suppression on Ji Ping. However, Ji Ping pulled together the three *Huan* and defeated Duke Zhao. As a result, Duke Zhao fled to Qi and died there. His throne was succeeded by his younger brother — Duke Ding. In the fifth year during his reign, Ji Ping died, leaving his chair to Ji Huan.

The Ji clan held the power of Lu for several generations, making the Duke of Lu a puppet. Ridiculously, despite his powers, Ji Huan always felt the threat from his own aggressive retainers just like he himself menacing Duke Ding. Moreover, his three retainers, Zhongliang Huai, Yang Huo and Gongshan Buniu, were involved in overt and covert struggles for the dominance of powers. When Zhongliang Huai had conflicts with Yang Huo, Gongshan Buniu showed up to mediate. However, Zhongliang Huai became even swollen with arrogance and was imprisoned by Yang Huo.

Ji Huan could not stand the situation and intervened, but was ignored by Yang Huo. Yang Huo even imprisoned Ji Huan until he gave up. In Confucius' eyes, all such turmoil was going against Zhou rites. Therefore, when Yang Huo intended to enhance his prestige and offered an audience with Confucius at his home, Confucius turned it down immediately.

As the one who could hold the Ji clan in control, Yang Huo would not give it up so easily. Thus he dispatched someone to present Confucius a braised piglet. According to the rites of the time, one who received gifts should return thanks by making a visit. That way, Yang Huo was confident that Confucius would visit him. Confucius was thus caught in a dilemma either visiting Yang Huo or not. But how to make the best of both options? Confucius then worked out a way: he chose a time to visit when Yang Huo was not at home.

But as the saying goes — "Chance contrives better than we ourselves": On his way, Confucius chanced upon Yang Huo.

Yang Huo started first, "Come on, I have something to say." Yang Huo might have figured out Confucius' purpose, and his tone already became unfriendly. "Could it be regarded as being benevolent for one who has talents but remains blind to state affairs?"

Knowing what he meant, Confucius said firmly, "No."

Yang Huo went on, "Could it be regarded as being wise for one who has a mind for politics but misses his chances?"

With his firmness, Confucius said, "No."

Having gained his upper hand, Yang Huo became more straightforward, "The days and months are passing away; the years do not wait for us."

Confucius kept struggling to revive Zhou rites. On the one hand he would not do anything to violate the rites; while on the other he had to safeguard himself in the chaos. Therefore, Confucius followed the intention of Yang Huo, saying, "Yes, I shall assume a public office." Actually, Confucius was just taking an expedient. When Yang Huo was defeated in a fight later and fled to the State of Qi, the whole thing ended up with nothing specific.

Besides Yang Huo, there was another aggressive retainer named Gongshan Buniu in the Ji Huan's clan. This man learned no lesson from Zhongliang Huai and Yang Huo. When he captured a place called Fei in Lu in 501BC, Gongshan Buniu attempted to contend against Ji Huan. He also summoned Confucius and Confucius planned to see him. Rather displeased, his disciple Zi Lu said, "It's better not to have a place to go, but why bother meeting such a man?" Confucius said, "Would I be summoned without a reason? If I am offered an office, I would work to revive the Zhou glories."

For his disciples, they surely could not understand why the Master rejected Yang Huo but accepted Gongshan Buniu. As a matter of fact, Confucius had some expectation on another man named Fo Xi besides Gongshan Buniu. Fo Xi was the fief chief under Zhao Jian, a *Dafu* in the State of Jin. Fo Xi took a place called Zhong Mou as his foothold to fight against Zhao Jian. He too made an offer to Confucius and Confucius planned to meet him.

On that Zi Lu questioned again, "I have heard from you before that 'a gentleman does not befriend one who did evil deeds'. But now Fo Xi has occupied Zhong Mou and wants to revolt. Then what's the point if you are going to join him?"

"Truly," Confucius explained, "I have said that. But have you not heard, 'Those that are truly hard could never be ground thin' or 'Those that are truly white could never be stained black'. Would I want to be like a gourd, only hung but never eaten?"

Confucius explained that he would not change his standpoint in a chaotic time. Meanwhile, a true gentleman should not only aim to preserve his own integrity in chaos, but try to make reforms. To quote himself, "If the Way exists, it is unnecessary for me to change it." It was just because the lack of the Way that Confucius had to participate actively to initiate reforms. To Confucius, Gongshan and Fo Xi were revolting, but that might turn out to be a starting point to revive Zhou rites if he could change them.

Caught in a dilemma, Confucius eventually went nowhere. All were fighting against each other: the dukes wanted to overthrow their common ruler; the ministers wanted to contain their dukes; the retainers wanted powers. Would Gongshan and Fo Xi follow his reforms? Would the insurrections be put down? Would Zhou rites thrive from grassroots? It was no wonder that Confucius should be caught in a dilemma. It is said that Confucius lacked understanding for his times, but that might be too partial.

29. 孔子劝学

子贡是孔子的高材生，很受孔子喜欢。可是有一天，子贡精神不振地跟孔子说："老师，我很累，我想休息，总是学习学习学习，我已经厌倦了。我不想再学习了。"老师问他不学习去做什么。子贡说："我要去侍奉君主。"老师微微一笑，"你忘了《诗》上说的，'从早到晚都要用温和而且恭敬的态度去料理所负责的事务，要谨慎也要严格。'你以为侍奉君子很容易吗？侍奉君主其实非常繁难，你怎么可以得到休息呢？"

子贡愣了愣，想了想，"那么我就去侍奉父母吧，这样总可以得到休息了吧？"

老师还是微微笑着，说："你忘了《诗》上说，'孝顺父母，不敢荒废不努力的孩子，才会得到上天的赏赐。'侍奉父母也是很繁难的事情，你怎么可以得到休息呢？"

子贡又愣住了。心里暗暗叹气，是啊，这些学过的东西我怎么都不记得了呢。但无论如何，我还是不想学习了。侍奉君主和父母都很繁难，那么待在家里跟妻子孩子在一起，总该可以得到休息了吧。没想到跟老师一说，老师又笑了。“《诗》上说，要让自己的妻子做出榜样，还要推及到兄弟，这样整个国家才可以治理好。妻子、孩子、兄弟间的事情很是繁难的，你怎么得到休息呢？”

子贡急了，“那么我到朋友们中间去，他们该不会让我为难了。”

老师还是笑了，“《诗》上说，朋友们彼此之间应该互相帮助，要使得大家用严肃的心情来相互支持。朋友之间也有繁难，你怎么能因此得到休息呢？”

子贡心里叹服着老师的博学与智慧，嘴里却还要强辩：“那大不了让我去乡村耕种，这样总行了吧？反正不管怎样，我是不要读书了。”

老师还是没同意子贡，“你不记得《诗》里说，白天你得去打茅草，晚上你得去搓草绳，房子要赶快盖好，回头马上得下地播种各种农作物。白天黑夜，春夏秋冬都有忙不完的活，你怎么得到休息？”

这下，子贡沮丧了，无可奈何地看着老师，“这么说我就找不到可以休息的机会了？”

“有啊，”老师指指远处，“你看那边那高高隆起的坟墓，那么高，那么大，那才是个休息的好去处。”

子贡明白了。

“活到老，学到老，” 人的一生都在求索，在追寻，没什么时间可以休息。这是一种积极的人生态度，但不是每个人都这样。德国哲学家叔本华就讲，人生是痛苦无聊的过程，就像钟摆不停地摇晃，毫无疑义，摆脱痛苦的最好办法是停止追求。叔本华与孔子形成了鲜明的对照。

CONFUCIUS PERSUADING PEOPLE TO STUDY

Zi Gong, a gifted student of Confucius, was favored by the Master. One day, Zi Gong said to Confucius in low spirit, "Master, I am really tired and want to have a rest. Study, study and study! I am fed up. I do not want to study any longer." The Master asked him what he would do if he did not study. Zi Gong answered, "I would serve the ruler." Confucius smiled, "You've forgotten what is said in *The Book of Odes*, 'You must do things you are in charge of gently and reverently day and night. You should be careful and rigid.' Do you think it is an easy job to serve the ruler? It is difficult and tiring. How could you rest?"

Zi Gong became speechless for a while, and then said, "Then I would serve my parents, and I can get a rest!"

The Master smiled again, "You've forgotten what *The Book of Odes* says, 'Being dutiful to the parents means not to idle away, and only such kind of person would be rewarded'. It is also tiring and difficult to serve the parents. How could you rest?"

Zi Gong felt stunned and sighed secretly, speaking to himself, "Yes, all these I have learned and how could I have forgotten them all. But anyway, I do not want to study any more. If it is tiring and difficult to serve the ruler or my parents, I would stay at home with my wife and kids, and I can rest." But when he told the Master, the Master smiled, "*The Book of Odes* tells us we should help the wife to be an example and our brothers to be examples as well, and the whole state could be well governed. It is difficult to deal with the affairs concerning of the wife and the brothers. How could you rest?"

Zi Gong was tired out and said, "Then I would go to my friends. They would not trouble me."

Again, the Master said with a smile, "*The Book of Odes* says friends should help each other, treat each other seriously and support each other sincerely. Difficulties also exist among the contact with friends. How could you rest?"

Zi Gong gasped in admiration for his Master's learning and wisdom, but still argued, "Then for the worst, I could farm in the countryside. Would that work? No matter how it might be, I would not study."

The Master still disagreed, "Have you forgotten what *The Book of Odes* says — you have to cut grass in the day and to make hay rolls at night. You are in a hurry to build your house and run among the fields to plant grains. You are busy with all the labor work from day to night throughout the four seasons. How could you rest?"

Zi Gong was in desperation and looked at his Master helplessly, "Then I could never have the chance to rest?"

"Yes," said the Master, "look at the high tombs over there, high and big. That's a good place to rest."

Eventually Zi Gong understood.

"Live and learn!" It is a positive attitude toward life that we should pursue throughout the life, finding no time to rest. However, not everyone shares Confucius' views. For example, the German philosopher Schopenhauer once said life was a boring and painful journey like the pendulum that kept swaying, and sure enough, the best way to get rid of the suffering was to stop pursuing. Schopenhauer and Confucius have made a world of difference towards life.

30. 丑陋的哀骀它

卫国有个奇丑无比的人，叫哀骀它。但是这个丑人有无比的魅力，男人跟他在一起，就会眷恋他不愿离开；女人见了他，就回家乞求父母说“与其做别人的妻子，不如给他当妾”，这样的女人有十多个呢！

鲁国国王鲁哀公听说后很诧异，就把他召到鲁国来见面。这一看，果然是丑得足以令天下人惊骇！然而，不到一个月，鲁哀公就喜欢上了他的为人；不到一年，鲁哀公就对他深信不疑了。当时鲁国缺乏宰相，哀公就把国事都托付给他。哀骀它好像懵里懵懂，过后才反应过来他是宰相了，有些心不在焉，想要推辞。哀公以为他不满意只是做个宰相，也觉得挺惭愧的，就要把整个国家都给他。没想到过不了多久哀骀它就走了。这一走，哀公忧郁苦闷得很，好像失去了宝贝，好像国内再没有可以一同快乐的人了。

鲁哀公左想右想，不知道自己怎么了，为什么对这个奇丑的人这么念念不忘。他请来孔子，问孔子这个哀骀它是个什么样的人。

孔子讲了个小故事：他有次出使楚国，路上碰到一群小猪和一只母猪。那只母猪显然刚刚死去，而那些猪娃娃们都不知道，还在吸吮妈妈的奶汁。可是，过了一会儿之后，这些小猪都惊恐起来了，纷纷离开母猪逃走了。因为他们发现这个妈妈已经变了，不再照顾自己，不再温暖自己，跟以前不一样了。所以，小猪们围绕在猪妈妈身边，爱着自己的母亲的时候，不是因为妈妈的外表形体，而是因为妈妈的精神，支配着形体的精神。妈妈死了，形体依旧，可是精神没有了，于是，猪娃娃们不得不离开。

那些离不开哀骀它的男人，那些想嫁给哀骀它的女人，还有这个因为哀骀它的离开而失魂落魄的鲁哀公，面对着哀骀它这样的丑陋面孔，却都醉心于他那美妙的精神世界。孔子评价他是个才智皆备的人，具有完美修养的人，使得人们都不愿离开他。

孔子是爱美的，但他更看重善。他评价舜时代的《韶乐》，说是“尽美”“尽善”；而武王时代的《武乐》，却是“尽美”而“未尽善”。孔子认为小猪都能辨别精神与外表的不同作用，况且人呢！然而，孔子也一针见血地指出：“吾未见好德如好色者也。”从人的本能来说，爱好美色是自然的，风花雪月、良辰美景、美女俊男，总是让人欲罢不能。现代社会，求职要扮靓，卖车要美女车模，全球在选美。爱美之心，无可厚非，但人类之所以有别于动物，是因为人类能以德来修正先天的不足。天然美好的身躯与面庞，如果没有品德的光芒，也不能长久地拥有光彩。美色养眼，美德养心。当内心的美和外在的美不能兼得时，我们选择的是后者，因为一个人失去眼还能活，失去心则必死。

THE UGLY AITAI TUO

There was an ugly man in the State of Wei, called Aitai Tuo. Though ugly, this man had unique charms. When a man had stayed with him, he would have an attachment to him and could not stay away. When a woman met him, she would present to her parents, saying, "I would rather be his concubine than a wife of any others." And women like that are more than ten.

After hearing of that, Duke Ai of Lu felt surprised, and summoned the man to Lu for an audience. He did look ugly to frighten anyone under Heaven. However, before barely a month, Duke Ai had already come to take a liking for him. Before one year had passed, Duke Ai had already trusted him without a shadow of doubt. When the prime minister's office was vacant in Lu, Duke Ai entrusted Aitai Tuo all the state affairs. However, it seemed that Aitai Tuo was too ignorant to realize that he was put to the chair of the prime minister, and intended to decline the offer. Duke Ai took it that he was not interested, and would even entrust him the whole state. In a little time, Aitai Tuo left the State of Lu, leaving Duke Ai in frustration. He seemed to have lost a valuable treasure and could find no others in his state to share his joys.

All thoughts having revolved in his mind, Duke Ai could figure out no reason for his addiction to this ugly man. He then had Confucius over to ask about Aitai Tuo.

Confucius told the duke a story. Once he went on a mission to the State of Chu. On the way he came across a herd of piglets and a sow. Obviously the sow had just died. The piglets, however, did not realize that and continued to suck for milk. In a short while, the piglets became frightened and ran away, for they had found their mom becoming different and no longer cared them with her warmth. In fact, what they had loved in their mom was not her bodily figure, but what had given animation to her figure. But after she died, there was no more such animation and the piglets had to leave.

Be it the men, the ladies, or Duke Ai, they indulged themselves in the wonderful spiritual world despite his ugly looks. Thus Confucius praised Aitai Tuo as one with ability and wisdom and ultimate integrity, making everyone reluctant to leave him.

Confucius had a taste for beauty, but he thought more of kindness. He remarked that the *Shao Yue* music of the Shun era had reached the perfection of "beauty" and "kindness". The *Wu Yue* music of King Wu's time, however, achieved the perfection of "beauty" but not "kindness". To Confucius, even the piglets could differentiate the spirit from the bodily figure, let alone the human beings. Meanwhile, Confucius made a pointed remark that "I have not seen one who loves virtue as he loves beauty."

Man loves beauty by instinct. The beautiful scenery of wind, flower, snow, moon, charming belles or handsome lads — all these would make it hard for one to part with. In our society, one has to dress up for job hunting. Beauties are a must on a car fair. There is Miss Here and There throughout the world. There is no ground for blaming the men that have a love for the beautiful. What differentiates the human beings from the animals lies in the fact that human beings could rectify their inherent shortages with virtues. A born beauty would not shine long if virtueless. The beautiful feasts our eyes, but the virtuous feasts our heart. When the two could not be balanced, we would choose virtues, for we survive without eyes but die a sure death without the heart.

31. 重外物则内心拙

有一次颜渊要渡过一条宽阔的大河，他找了一条船，让船老大撑船送他过去。船老大驾船如神，在汹涌的波浪中穿梭自如，面色平静，动作协调有力，就像走在平地上一样轻松自在。颜渊看着十分惊异。他忍不住问船老大："像你这样的驾船本领能学会吗？"船老大的回答也很让颜渊吃惊："当然能学。如果是擅长游泳的人，只要经过数次练习就能学会。如果是擅长潜泳的人，那就是没见过船也会驾驶。"颜渊无法理解，不相信学会驾船会这么容易。他又问船老大，船老大却怎么也不肯说了。

过了河以后，颜渊满腹疑问。一见到老师立刻就把心中的疑惑说了出来，问老师是怎么回事。老师略一思索就把道理讲给颜渊听："擅长游泳的人练习数次就能学会，因为他不会老想着这是在水里，会有危险。在他眼里水路和泥路没什么区别。说擅长潜泳的人即便没见过船也能驾船，是因为他觉得深渊就像陆上的土丘，即便是翻船，也不过就像是车子从土丘上滑落下来，不用担忧，甚至觉得就像游戏。假使上万艘船只翻覆的惨状摆在他的面前，他也不会恐惧，不会受到惊扰，他的内心依旧会悠然自得。因为水对于他而言，就像空气，他与水融为一体，无论是漩涡还是暗礁，他都不会惧怕。”

老师停顿了一下，又说：“当我们把瓦片作为赌注的时候，我们会掷射得很准，因为我们不会把它放在心里；一旦用带钩（一种贵重的东西）作赌注，心里就有恐惧，就会有得失的考虑；而用黄金作赌注的时候，头脑就会昏乱。事实上他的掷射技巧是一样的，但心中想的不同。一看重带钩，看重黄金，他的内心就会笨拙；当他心中无物的时候，内心就会轻快。驾船的道理就是这样的。”

一些优秀运动员，在平时的训练中表现非常出色。当他走向竞赛场地，处身群情激昂的氛围中时，那块金牌，那个金杯，那只金靴，那条绶带，都会变成沉甸甸的砖石，重重地压在他的心里。于是，弹跳不再富有弹性，运球突破不再敏捷准确，投篮不再百发百中，扣杀不再强劲有力。当一个人能够不受外物干扰的时候，他的内心才会灵巧有力。

EXTERNAL ATTENTION CAUSES INTERNAL TENSION

Yan Yuan was once to cross a wide river. He found a boat and had the ferryman to pilot. As if with magic, the man maneuvered his boat skillfully through the surging waves. He was at such ease and so calm and balanced in his powerful moves that he was just like walking on a flat land. Rather amazed, Yan Yuan couldn't help asking him, “Could your management of boat be learned?” Quite beyond his expectation, the man said, "Yes, it may! Good swimmers can learn it quickly; but as for divers, without having seen a boat, they can manage it at once." That was too much for Yan Yuan to comprehend as he could not believe it was such an easy job. He tried to ask further, but the man kept his mouth shut.

After he alighted the boat, Yan Yuan was filled with suspicion. When he came to Confucius, he told the whole story and asked the reason. Without much thinking, the Master said, "Good swimmers acquire the ability quickly — they forget the water (and its dangers) and sees no difference between a waterway and a land road. As to those who are able to dive, they are able to manage it at once. They look on the river as if it were a hill-side, and the upsetting of a boat as the going back of a carriage. Even at the sight of thousands of boats in wreckage, he would not fear or feel disturbed but remain at leisure. To him the water is of no difference from the air, and he has no fear for swirls or hidden reefs."

With a pause, the Master continued, "When we are contending for a piece of earthenware, we put forth all our skills as we do not care for the earthenware itself. If the prize is a buckle of brass, we shoot timorously as we become mindful of the loss. If the prize is an article of gold, we shoot in a messy dizziness. Our skills are the same in all the cases, but we are influenced by different thoughts. When the thought of brass or gold captures our mind, we feel resourceless in our heart. We can feel at ease when there is nothing to trouble our heart. That's the truth of the boat riding."

There are athletes who demonstrate excellent performance in their training. When he walks into the court in a fevered atmosphere, however, he would have a heavy pressure with the thought of the gold medal, the cup, the boots, or the ribbon. Thus he would be less agile in his jumping; or not as nimble while dribbling along the basketball court; or less accurate in his shooting; or less powerful in his spikes. It is only when one does not feel disturbed by external forces that could he remain as agile and powerful as he is.

32. 真恩真义和假恩假义

孔子在卫国呆了很长一段时间后，还是没有得到任用。他很失望，打算离开卫国去晋国见赵简子。

他带着弟子们走到黄河边时，听说了窦鸣犊、舜华的死讯。于是他面对着黄河感慨地说："真是壮美啊，这浩浩荡荡的河水！我不能过河了，这是命运啊！"

子贡听他这么说，恭恭敬敬地走上前，问到："请问老师你这么说是什么意思？"

孔子说："窦鸣犊、舜华这两位是晋国非常贤能的臣子，赵简子没有得志的时候，靠着这两个人才做了官。可现在他已经得了志，却还不满足，杀了这两个人来做更大的官。我听说，谁要是剖腹取胎或者杀死刚刚出生的禽兽，那么麒麟就不会在他的城邑郊外出现；谁要是抽干池里的水来捕鱼，那么蛟龙就不会再呆在他那儿的深渊来调和阴阳，兴云作雨；谁要是毁坏鸟窝，打破鸟蛋，那么凤凰就不会在他的城邑上空飞翔。为什么呢？这是因为有道德的人忌讳伤害他的同类。你看，连鸟兽都尚且知道躲避不义的事情，何况我孔丘呢？”于是孔子带着弟子们到卫国和晋国交界处的陬乡休息，作了一首琴曲《陬操》，哀悼窦鸣犊、舜华的惨死。

赵简子是个忘恩负义的人。在孔子眼里，这样的人连禽兽都不如。但是孔子眼里的恩和义，绝不是狭隘的私人恩义。鲁国大夫叔孙穆子为了避难逃奔到齐国，路上在一个叫庚宗的地方住宿。那个地方有个寡妇和穆子私通，生了个孩子叫牛。多年以后，穆子返回鲁国，让这个长大了的孩子牛负责家政。牛却总在穆子跟前说穆子的两个嫡子孟丙、仲壬的坏话，并找了个借口把他俩杀了。后来穆子生了病，牛也不送食物给父亲吃，直到穆子被饿死。穆子死后，牛辅佐穆子的一个叫昭子的庶子，把昭子立为叔孙氏的继承人。而这个昭子一即位，就召见家族成员，对他们说：“牛害了叔孙氏，搞乱了重要的正常秩序，杀嫡立庶，又分割封邑来行贿，想用这个方法来逃避罪责，没有比这更大的罪行了！一定要赶紧杀掉他！”于是，辅佐了昭子上台的牛反而被昭子杀死了。

孔子对这件事的评价，完全不同于赵简子杀了扶持过他的窦鸣犊和舜华这件事。孔子反而赞扬昭子，说：“叔孙昭子不把拥立自己看作牛的功劳，这对一般的人来说是不可能做到的。古贤人周任说过：为政的人不应该赏赐只对个人有私功的人，也不应该惩罚只对个人有私怨的人。《诗》上说，如果有正直的德行，天下四方的人都会顺从。这个叔孙昭子就具有这样的德行。”可见，孔子对叔孙昭子杀牛这件事的评价是很高的。孔子的看法很明确，从个人私利出发的言行不是为政之道，因为政者，正也。

TRUTHFUL AND FALSE GRATITUDE

After staying for quite a long period in the State of Wei, Confucius became frustrated for not receiving any royal appointment at all. He planned to leave Wei for the State of Jin to meet Zhao Jianzi.

When Confucius and his disciples reached the Yellow River, they heard of the death of Dou Mingdu and Shun Hua. Facing the river, Confucius sighed, "How marvelous the river is! See the rolling waves! It's all predestined that I cannot cross this river!"

Hearing that, Zi Gong walked up respectfully, asking, "Master, what does that mean?"

Confucius told him, "Dou Mingdu and Shun Hua had been respectably virtuous and talented ministers. Before Zhao Jianzi was up, he secured his career with the support from the two. Now he is up, but he is not contented and aiming higher position by killing the two. I have heard if one cuts open the belly for the fetus or kills the newly-born animal, the unicorn would no longer show up in the outskirts of his city; if one drains the pond to catch fish, the dragon would not stay to stir up rains to unite the *Yin* and *Yang*; if one ruins the bird's nest and breaks her eggs, there would be no phoenix to fly over his fief. Then why? It's because a virtuous man abstains from hurting his fellows. You see even birds and beasts would avoid the unjustified deeds, let alone I Confucius."

So Confucius led his disciples to a nearby village of Zou along the borders of Wei and Jin. There Confucius composed zither music *Melody of Zou* to express his condolences for the death of Dou Mingdu and Shun Hua.

Ungrateful and treacherous as he was, Zhao Jianzi amounted not even to a beast in the eyes of Confucius. Confucius' version of gratitude, however, was not a personal one in its narrow sense.

Sun Muzi was a *Dafu* in the court of Lu. He fled the chaos in Lu to Qi. On his way, Sun Muzi lodged in a place named Gengzong, and had an illicit relation with a widow there. Later, the widow gave birth to a son called Niu. Many years had passed before Sun Muzi returned to Lu, and had the grown-up Niu to be his home steward. However, Niu kept badmouthing the other two sons of Muzi's legal wife, Meng Bing and Zhong Ren, and eventually killed them on some pretexts. When Muzi fell ill, Niu did not even serve him food until he starved to death.

Niu then assisted Zhaozi, a son of Muzi from one of his concubines, and established him as the heir to the family. By the time Zhaozi took over the chair, he summoned the whole family and declared, "It was Niu that killed Muzi, and disturbed the set orders. He killed the orthodox sons and assisted one that did not come along on the major line. He had fragmented the family fief to bribe others in the hope to avoid responsibilities for his crimes. There could be no worse crime than this, and he is to be executed right away!" Therefore, he who assisted Zhaozi up to the chair received his doom from the assisted.

Confucius' comment on this was dramatically different from the one on Zhao Jianzi who killed Dou Mingdu and Shun Hua. On the contrary, Confucius sang high praises for Zhaozi, "Shusun Zhaozi did not take Niu's assistance as his merit, and that was not something average people could do. The ancient saint Zhou Ren had said: One who governs should not reward those who made private contributions, or punish those who had private grievance. In the *Book of Odes*, it reads: 'If the ruler has upright virtues, everyone in the four corners under Heaven follows.' This Shusun Zhaozi was one with such virtues." Therefore, we can see Confucius had high opinion for Zhaozi to kill Niu, as he was rather clear with his stand: the words and deeds out of personal interests should not be on the track of governance, or to quote himself, "To govern is to remain upright."

33. 眼见一定为实吗

孔子和他的弟子们被困在陈国和楚国交界处的时候，一连七天没吃上饭，大家都饿得受不了了，但又没办法。子贡是做生意的，随身携带的东西多少比别人多一点好一点，他拿了些东西想办法逃出去，找百姓换了些米。颜回和子路负责在人家废弃的破屋子里做饭。子路去打水，留下颜回一人。这时破屋子顶上掉下来一些尘土，偏偏都掉进了饭锅里。颜回便把那些沾了尘土的米饭抓出来放嘴里吃了。打水回来的子路恰好看到颜回往嘴里塞米饭，他非常生气，没想到颜回居然会趁大家都不在偷吃——谁不饿啊？子路很不高兴地去了老师那儿，气哼哼地问："难道一个仁人君子也会因为遭遇逆境而改变自己的气节吗？"

老师觉得很突然，不知道他的问题从何而来，但还是回答了："如果他已经改变了自己的气节，怎么还能被称为君子呢？”

“那么像颜回这样的人是不是会改变呢？”子路继续问。

孔子愣了一下，但很坚决地回答：“不会”。

子路见老师如此坚定，就把刚才看到的事情一五一十都说了。

孔子说：“我相信颜回是一个真君子，这已经很久了；但你所说的，我也不好怀疑。也许他那么做是事出有因。你等一等，我来问问他。”

孔子叫来颜回，对他说：“我刚才梦见我的先父了，他似乎在预示我什么。你把做好的饭给我，我想祭祀我的先父。”

颜回赶紧回答说：“不行，刚才饭里落进尘土了，如果留在那里，那太不干净了。如果扔了，那太可惜了。所以我就吃了那些脏的饭，不能用来祭祀了。”

孔子说：“那好吧，我也来吃吧。”

颜回走了。孔子对其他几个学生说：“我相信颜回，不是从今天开始的。”子路等几个人由此信服了。

这件事在《吕氏春秋·任数》里也有记载，但有些不同。《吕氏春秋》里记载的是孔子自己亲眼看见颜回在吃米饭。待将事情的前因后果弄清楚后，孔子忍不住感叹说：“可以信赖的应该算是眼睛了，可有时候眼睛还是不可信；可以依靠的应该算是心了，可有时候心也还是不足以依靠。你们要记得啊，真正了解一个人本来就很不容易的。”

我们常说“口说无凭，眼见为实”，这个故事里，不管是子路看见的，还是孔子自己看见的，都是亲眼所见，但他们见到的并非事实真相，他们的眼睛欺骗了他们，就如同我们看魔术表演的时候一样，明明看到的是这样的，事实上却根本不是这么回事，看来眼见不一定为实。当我们发现眼睛不足以明鉴事实的时候，孔子说要靠“心”。要用心去了解一个人。以长时间的心的交流为基础，把所见所闻建立在对一个人的了解、信任之上，就不会轻易被眼睛欺骗被耳朵蛊惑了。

IS SEEING REALLY BELIEVING?

When Confucius and his disciples were besieged at the border of Chen and Chu, they had run out of provisions for seven days in a row but were incapable of any action. As Zi Gong had his business, his personal belongings were somewhat better than others. Therefore, he selected some and fled out of the siege to exchange for some rice from the local peasants. Now in a deserted broken house, Yan Hui and Zi Lu were in charge of cooking. Zi Lu went out for water, leaving Yan Hui alone. It happened that some dusts on the ceiling fell into the cooking pot, so Yan Hui scratched the polluted rice and ate it. At that moment, Zi Lu returned and caught sight of that. And he became very angry: everyone was starving, but how could this Yan Hui reach out behind others! And so, Zi Lu went to his Master in a huff, saying, "Master, would a virtuous man compromise his integrity in adversity?"

Taken by surprise, Confucius had no idea why Zi Lu had such a question, but said, "If he had compromised, how could he still be called a gentleman?"

"Then could a gentleman like Yan Hui compromise?" Zi Lu continued.

With a brief pause, Confucius said firmly, "No!"

Seeing the master so confirmative, Zi Lu told him what he had seen just now.

Confucius said, "I trust the virtues of Yan Hui for long. But I cannot say no to what you have seen. Perhaps he had a reason for that. Take it easy, I would find it out."

Confucius summoned Yan Hui over, asking "I have just dreamt my late father. He was somehow showing me something. Now, give me the rice you have made, and I need make a sacrifice."

In haste, Yan Hui said, "No, dusts fell into the rice just now. If they are kept there, it would be too dirty. If dumping the rice, it would be too much a waste. Thus I ate the polluted rice, and they cannot be used for sacrifice."

Confucius said, "That's all right. Then I would like to join you to eat it."

After Yan Hui left, Confucius told his disciples, "I trust Yan Hui not just from today." From then on, Zi Lu and his fellows were convinced.

This story was also recorded in "Conforming to the Heavenly Way" of the *Spring and Autumn Annals of Lü Buwei*, though with certain variations. In this record, it was Confucius himself that was seeing Yan Hui eating the rice. After learning the whole issue, Confucius sighed, "We always feel we can trust our eyes for what we see. But sometimes it is not so. Perhaps it is our heart that is trustworthy. But that is not always the case either. Now remember, you young people, it is truly hard to learn a person!"

We always quote the saying, "Verbal statements are no guarantee, but seeing is believing." In this story, however, no matter whether Zi Lu or Confucius had seen with his own eyes, he did not see the truth, but was deceived by his eyes. It's just like the magic show we see — what comes to our eyes are not what they actually are. That seems to have falsified "seeing is believing". When we realize our eyes are not enough to identify the truth, we need to see with what Confucius called "heart" or our mind's eye so as to understand a person. With the exchanges of our hearts for a long time, we could therefore build up our "believing" on the understanding and trust we have on others, and would not be deceived by the "seeing" or "hearing".

34. 曾参挨打又挨批

曾参在家里跟父亲一起干农活，在瓜地里除草。可能是心思还在书本上，曾参一锄子下去草没除掉，却把瓜秧子的根锄断了。父亲曾皙大怒，“让你干点儿活你却尽添乱，成事不足，败事有余。”也不知道那天曾皙怎么了，火气大得冲天，骂完了还不解气，随手操了根木棍就开始打儿子。曾参一声不吭，没有辩解，也不躲闪，很快就被父亲打晕，倒在地上，过了好一会儿才醒过来。清醒过来后马上就爬起来，恭敬地对父亲说：“刚才我做错了事，让您生气了。您用力教训我，应该没累坏吧？”见父亲还是气哼哼的，他就慢慢地退下去，在屏风后面弹起琴唱起歌，希望父亲听到他的歌声后，知道儿子已经好了，没事儿了，好让他自己平静下来。

鲁国人听说曾参这样孝顺父亲，都称赞他懂事明理。偏偏孔子听说这件事情后，就跟门人说：“要是曾参来了，别让他进来。”曾参得知老师这样对待自己，觉得很奇怪。他觉得自己一点儿错也没有，便派人来向老师谢罪，其实是想知道老师为什么不要见他。

孔子对来人说："你没听说过以前舜是怎样做儿子的吗？他父亲是个瞎老头子，只要父亲要他做事，从没有叫不到他的时候，总是侍奉在父亲身边，一叫就应。一旦父亲暴怒，想要抓住他杀他，他就逃得远远的，从不让父亲抓到。如果父亲用小棍子打他，他就随父亲打，不躲避；但如果父亲用大棍子打他，他就躲开。可看看你，在父亲暴怒的时候，你乖乖地把自己送上去，站在那里一动不动。万一父亲盛怒之下，一失手真的把你打死了，你父亲不就成了罪犯？你说你这样做是孝还是不孝？再说你也是天子的臣民，你父亲杀了你，就是杀死天子的臣民，这样的罪名你难道不知道会是怎样的结果？"

孔子看问题总是比常人要更深一层。当曾参自以为自己是大孝子，当邻里乡亲也在夸赞曾参的孝顺时，只有孔子看到了更严峻的一方面——父亲杀死儿子同样是犯罪。如果儿子任其棍打，便是给父亲制造了犯罪的条件——孝顺还是不孝顺，不能简单地以是否顺从来衡量。小辈应该让长辈欢心，也应该制止长辈不恰当的言论或者行为。

其实，不论是小辈对长辈，还是邻里之间，朋友之间，都不能把温顺作为调解、处理彼此关系的唯一方法。小事我们提倡互相包容谦让，但涉及原则性的事情，我们都必须做出正确的选择与判断，不能因为有亲密的关系就不劝阻不批判，隐瞒、包庇错误的言行，将会导致更大的错误的发生。

ZENG SHEN BEING BEATEN AND CRITICIZED

One day, Zeng Shen was weeding in the melon field with his father. It might be that his thoughts were still on his books, and with a hoe he snapped some seedling roots. Fuming with anger, his father Zeng Xi roared, "When I get you to the fields, you are only good at making troubles. You, just worse than a good-for-nothing!" For strange reasons, Zeng Xi was unusually angry that day and it was not enough to vent his anger with mere scolding. He picked up a club and beat his son.

Zeng Shen remained silent. He did not argue or duck his father's clubs. Soon he was stunned and fell to the ground. After quite a while when he came to himself, Zeng Shen said respectfully to his father, "I have made a mistake just now and led to your anger. And it must have cost your energy when educating me. I hope that has not tired you." Seeing that his father was still angry, Zeng Shen withdrew himself slowly to the back of the screen, and sang to his zither. He hoped that would make his father know he was fine and thus could calm down.

People in the State of Lu heard of the filial son, and praised him for understanding the proprieties. Confucius, however, told his disciples, "When Zeng Shen visits me, keep him out." After learning that, Zeng Shen felt confused. He thought he had done nothing wrong. Thus he sent someone to offer his apology to his master, and tried to figure out why his master did not want to see him.

Confucius told the errand-runner, "Have you ever heard how Shun in previous times played his role of a son? His father was blind. Whenever his father wanted him, Shun was at his side. But when the old man was in a violent rage and wanted to kill his son, Shun would run away to avoid. When his father wanted to beat him with a small stick, he would bear it. But if his father had a big club, he would duck away. But now, look at yourself! You showed yourself up when your father was in such a rage, and you did not even move. What if your father was too angry and beat you to death. Were you making your own father a criminal? Now, is that filial of you or not? Moreover, you are a subject to the duke of the state. If your father had killed you, he was killing a subject of the duke's. Don't you realize the outcome of such a crime?"

Confucius would always see deeper on the questions. When Zeng Shen thought he was a dutiful son, and his neighbors sang their praises, Confucius had already seen a more serious aspect: it would be a crime for the father to kill his son. If the son let his father beat at his will, it was equal to make a crime possible for his father. It is not just obedience to seniors that makes one filial. The juniors have the obligation to make their seniors happy, but they should also check their inappropriate talks or deeds.

In fact, compliance should not be the only resort for the handling of interpersonal relationship, whether between juniors and seniors, among neighbors, or between friends. We encourage tolerance and modesty for trifles. But for matters of principles, we need discretion and dissuade or criticize despite our personal closeness. Otherwise, to disguise or cover up such talks or action would only lead to even serious mistakes.

35. 颜回输了帽子

颜回是孔子最看重的学生，非常爱学习，也很有悟性，品德高尚，连孔子自己都说比不上颜回。有一天，颜回出去办事，看见一家布店前围着很多人，吵吵嚷嚷。他看了一会儿，挤进去问原因，才知道是买布的跟卖布的发生了纠纷。

买布的大嚷大叫：“三八二十三，三八就是二十三，你为啥要我二十四个钱？”

颜回听了，走到买布的跟前，鞠了一躬，然后说：“这位大哥，三八是二十四，怎么会是二十三呢？是你算错了，不要吵啦。”买布的自然不服气，指着颜回的鼻子说：“你是谁？谁让你出来评理的？你说三八二十四就是二十四了？你算老几？要评理只有找孔夫子，错与不错只有他说了算！走，咱找他评理去！”

颜回见他火气很大，一下子也没办法让他平静下来，只好说：“那好吧。不过，孔夫子要是说你错了怎么办？”

买布的说：“说我错了，就把我的头输给你。那要是你错了呢？”颜回说：“要是说我错了，就把我的帽子(冠)输给你。”二人打着赌，找到了孔子。孔子问清楚了情况，对颜回笑笑说：“三八就是二十三哪！颜回，你输啦，把帽子取下来给人家吧！”

颜回从来不跟老师斗嘴。他听孔子说他错了，就老老实实摘下帽子，交给了买布的。那人接过帽子，得意洋洋地走了。对孔子的这次评判，颜回表面上绝对服从，心里却想不通。他认为孔子已经老糊涂，便不想再跟孔子学习了。

第二天，颜回说家中有事，要请假回去。孔子明白颜回的心事，也不点破，同意他回家。临走前，颜回去跟孔子告别。孔子要他办完家里的事情马上就回来，并嘱咐他两句话：“千年古树莫存身，杀人不明勿动手。”

颜回说了声“记住了”，便动身往家走。走到半路上，突然乌云滚滚，刮起大风，雷鸣电闪，眼看要下大雨。颜回看见路旁有棵大树，而且粗大的树干上裂了个大洞，刚好可以躲进一个人，他便钻进这棵大树的空树干里，想避避雨。正当他靠着树干坐下歇脚，他猛然想起走前孔子跟他说的“千年古树莫存身”的话，心想，师徒一场，再听他一次话吧，便又从空树干中走了出来。他刚离开没走多远，一个炸雷，把那棵古树劈断了。颜回大吃一惊：老师的第一句话应验啦！救了我的命。那他还说“杀人不明勿动手”，难道我还会杀人吗？

颜回边想边赶路，到家，已是深夜。他不想惊动家人，就用随身佩带的宝剑，拨开了妻子卧室的门栓。颜回走到床前一摸，啊呀呀，南头睡了一个人，北头也睡了一个人！他怒从心头起，举剑就要砍，还好，孔子的第二句话“杀人不明勿动手”猛地在脑海里闪了一下。他放下剑，点上灯一看，床上一头睡的是妻子，一头睡的是妹妹。

等天一亮，颜回就迫不及待地回到老师那儿去，见了孔子便跪下说：“老师，您那两句话，救了我、我妻子和我妹妹三个人哪！您事前怎么会知道要发生的事呢？”孔子把颜回扶起来说：“昨天天气燥热，估计会有雷雨，所以就提醒你“千年古树莫存身”。你又是带着气走的，身上还佩带着宝剑，所以我告诫你“杀人不明勿动手”。

颜回鞠躬说：“老师料事如神，学生十分敬佩！”

孔子又开导颜回说：“我知道你请假回家是假的，其实是以为我老糊涂了，不愿再跟我学习。你现在再想想，要是我说三八二十三是对的，你输了，不过只输个帽子；我要是说三八二十四是对的，便是他输了，那他可是要输给你脑袋，一条人命啊！你说帽子重要还是人命重要呢？”

颜回恍然大悟，“扑通”跪在孔子面前，说：“老师重大义而轻小是小非，学生还以为老师年纪大脑子欠清醒呢。学生惭愧万分！”从这以后，孔子无论去哪里，颜回都跟着，再也没离开过他。

姜还是老的辣。尽管买布人说“输了就不要脑袋了”可能只是句气话或者玩笑话，但孔子还是巧妙地化解了纠纷，并让颜回明白怎样更好地处理类似的问题——不是原则性的大是大非问题，不妨变通一下，能让双方取得一个双赢的结果，而不是两败俱伤。想想看，就算买布人真的输掉了脑袋，颜回又能得到什么呢？孔子这会儿判买布人赢了，买布人很快就会明白孔子判他赢的道理的。

YAN HUI LOSING HIS HAT

The most valued disciple as he was to Confucius, Yan Hui was diligent, competent at comprehension, and highly virtuous. Confucius himself even said he could not rival Yan Hui. One day, Yan Hui was running an errand, and on the way he passed a cloth store. A big noisy crowd gathered there. After watching a moment, Yan Hui elbowed his way in to ask what had happened, and learned the buyer was quarrelling with the storekeeper.

The buyer shouted, "Three times eight is twenty-three, exactly twenty-three. But why do you charge me twenty-four?

Hearing that, Yan Hui walked up and bowed to the man, saying, "My brother, three times eight should be twenty-four. But how could it be twenty-three? You made a wrong calculation. Now do not quarrel." Barely convinced, the buyer pointed his finger at Yan Hui, shouting, "Who are you? Who on earth have sent you here to be our judge? Is it twenty-four just because you said it? How senior are you? The only judge is Confucius. He has the say for right or wrong. Go, let's go to him for the answer!"

Seeing his temper so high, Yan Hui found no immediate way to calm him down but to say, "That's all right. But what if Confucius says you are wrong?"

"If I'm wrong," said the buyer, "I lose my head. Then what if you are wrong?"

"If I am wrong," said Yan Hui, "I lose my hat."

Holding their bet, the two men found Confucius. After learning the story, Confucius smiled to Yan Hui, "Ya, three times eight is twenty-three. Yan Hui, you have lost it. Now give your hat to him!"

Yan Hui never argued with his master and honestly took off his hat and gave it to the man. Rather delighted, the man walked away with the hat. Though having followed his master in the argument, Yan Hui could not figure out the reason. He came to think Confucius was too old to be wise any more, and had a mind to stay away from him.

The second day, Yan Hui asked for leave on the pretext of family business. Having already read his mind, Confucius did not point it out but agreed. Upon parting, Confucius required him to return when getting his family business done, and told him to note two things: "Never take shelter under an age-old tree. Never turn to the sword before making clear the truth."

With a "yes", Yan Hui took his leave. While in the mid way, the sky turned black, winds blew, lightening flashed, and thunder rolled. A storm was in the making. It happened there was a big tree at the roadside with a big crack in the trunk that was just right to shelter a person. Yan Hui hurriedly made his way into the crack and sat down for a rest. Suddenly the parting words of Confucius flashed through his mind: "Never take shelter under an age-old tree." Thinking these might be the last words he would follow his master, Yan Hui walked out of the crack. No sooner than he stepped out did an explosive thunder snap the tree. Shocked, Yan Hui realized his master's first message had become true, and had saved his life! Then he began wondering the second message "Never turn to the sword before making clear the truth" — was he going to kill someone?

Feeling puzzled all the way, Yan Hui hurried on with his journey. It was already late in the night when he got home. Not wanting to wake up his family, Yan Hui unlatched the door with his sword. He felt his way in the dark to the bedside only to touch two heads, one to the south and the other to the north. A sudden rage overtook him and he held up his sword. Before he hacked down, his master's second message flashed through his mind — "Never turn to the sword before making clear the truth." He laid down the sword and lit up the room. On the two ends in the bed were his wife and his younger sister.

When the next day broke, Yan Hui made his way back to Confucius. Falling on his knees before Confucius, Yan Hui said, "Master, you have saved the three of me, my wife and my younger sister with your two messages! But how could you have been such a prophet?"

Holding Yan Hui back to his feet, Confucius told him, "It was sultry yesterday, and I thought there could be a thunderstorm. Therefore I warned you not to take shelter under an age-old tree. You were leaving in anger, and with your sword. Therefore I warned you not to kill before making clear the truth."

Bowing in admiration, Yan Hui said, "Master, you foretell things with miraculous accuracy! I bosom nothing but admiration!"

Confucius continued to advise Yan Hui, saying, "I knew you were taking a false excuse to go home, but regarded me as being too old to be wise and would not follow me. Now, let's pick up the argument. When I said yes to twenty-three, you lost it, but just lost your hat. Should I have said yes to twenty-four, the man would have lost it, and he lost his head. But that's a life! Now between a hat and a head, which would you say is more important?"

Just like a light broke in upon him, Yan Hui fell on his knees again, saying, "Master, you held to the cardinal principles rather than trivialities, but what a terrible shame it was on me to take that you were getting on in age and becoming hazy on things." Henceforth, Yan Hui followed Confucius wherever he went.

The older the ginger, the more pungent its flavor: Though the buyer made the big bet on his head out of either his anger or just blaguing, Confucius tactfully solved the dispute and taught Yan Hui the principle to handle similar cases — be flexible upon things that were of no cardinal principles so as to achieve win-win results. It would make no sense to make both sides lose: what could Yan Hui have gained if the buyer had lost his head? Confucius said yes to the buyer, but the man would soon realize the truth later on.

36. 知之为知之，不知为不知

有一回，孔子到齐国去，路上看见两个小孩正在斗嘴，好像是在辩论什么问题，争得很激烈，谁也说服不了谁。

孔子看了，觉得挺有趣，就对跟在身后的学生子路说：“咱们过去听听孩子们在辩论什么，顺便歇歇脚，好不好？”子路有些不以为然，撇了撇嘴说：“两个黄毛小子能说出什么东西来？”

“呵呵，别小看孩子，每个人看世界的眼光都有他的道理，不分年龄大小。有时候，小孩子讲出的道理，比那些愚蠢自负的成年人要强得多呢！”子路一下子红了脸，没再说什么。

孔子走过去和蔼地跟孩子们说：“我叫孔丘，看见你们争辩得这么热烈，也想参加进来，你们看可不可以呀？”

“噢，原来你就是那个孔夫子呀，听说你很有学问。好吧，就请你来给我们评一评，看谁说得对！”一个孩子说。

孔子笑着说："好吧，你们一个一个地讲，别急。"

一个孩子说："我们在争论太阳什么时候离我们最近。我说早上近，他说中午近，你说说，是谁对呢？"孔子认真地想了一会儿说："这个问题我过去没考虑过，不敢随便乱讲，还是先请你们把各自理由讲一讲吧。"

一个孩子抢着说："你看，早上太阳又大又圆，可到了中午，太阳就变小了。我们谁都知道近的东西看起来大，远的东西看起来小。"

另一个孩子接着说："他说得不对，早上太阳凉飕飕的，一点儿也不热，因为它离我们太远了；可是到了中午，太阳却像开水一样烫人，这不就说明中午太阳离我们近吗？"

说完，两个孩子一齐看着孔子，忽闪忽闪的两双眼睛似乎在说："你来评评谁对吧。"

这下可把孔子难住了，他反复想了半天，还是觉得两个孩子各自都有道理，实在分不清谁对谁错。于是他老老实实地承认："这个问题我回答不了，以后我向更有学问的人请教一下，再来回答你们吧。"

两个孩子听后哈哈大笑："人家都说孔夫子是个圣人，原来你也回答不了我们的问题呀！"说完就转身跑了。

在一旁听着的子路很不服气地说："您真应该随便讲点什么，至少得把他们镇住。"

孔子说："不，如果不是老老实实地承认自己不懂，怎么能听到这番有趣的道理。在学习上，我们知道就说知道，不知道就说不知道。只有抱着这种诚实的态度，才能学到真正的知识。"

现在我们常用的成语"知之为知之，不知为不知"就是由此而来的，它要求做学问要有老实的态度，来不得半点儿虚假，还要善于学习，善于发现，即使是面对孩子。孩子对世界探索的眼光常常不同于成年人，对成年人习以为常、熟视无睹的问题，他们会从新的角度提出问题。尽管他们不能给你答案，但能启发你去思考。

TAKING WHAT IS KNOWN AS KNOWN

Confucius was once on his way to the State of Qi and met two kids bickering with each other. They seemed to be caught in an argument and no one could be convinced.

Feeling amused, Confucius summoned his disciples behind, saying, "Why not go and see what they are arguing? We might take a rest." With palpable contempt, Zi Lu said, "What could come out of the mouths of two kids?"

"Now, do not look down upon kids." Confucius turned to Zi Lu, "Everyone, young or old, has something in his views for the world. Sometimes, the kids have a way stronger argument than the stupid arrogant adults." Blushed, Zi Lu found no words.

Confucius walked up to the kids and asked them kindly, "My name is Kong Qiu. I see you arguing so eagerly. May I join you?"

"Oh, you are the well-known Confucius!" One of the kids turned to him, "I heard you know quite a lot. Come on, I would like to invite you to be our judge, and see who is right."

Smiling, Confucius said, "Sure! Now you take turns, but no rush."

So one started, saying, "We were arguing when the sun is nearest to us. I say it's early morning but he insists it's noon. Now you tell us, who is right?"

After thinking hard for a while, Confucius told them, "In fact, I have never given any thought to this question before. So I cannot take it for granted. But I would like to hear your reasoning first."

One kid could not wait, saying, "You see? In the morning the sun is big and round, but it becomes small at noon. We all know objects look big when they are close and small when far."

"No, he is wrong!" said the other, "In the morning the sun is chilly and not warm at all. That's because it's too far from us. At noon, it's hot like the hot water. So, can't that show it's closer to us at noon?"

After that, the two kids turned to Confucius, their eyes blinking with wonders like saying, "Would you be our judge now?"

Now Confucius was really puzzled. After thinking for a long while, he felt both the kids made a sense, but could not tell who was right. Thus he admitted to them, "I can't tell you now. But I will learn from the more learned and then I can answer you."

At that the two kids burst into laughter, "People say Confucius is a sage. But now you can't answer our questions!" Then they ran away.

Standing aside, Zi Lu felt rather unhappy, "Master, you might have told the kids something, at least to keep them quiet."

"No," Confucius told him, "If we do not admit honestly our lack of the knowledge, how could we have heard such an interesting argument? In learning, we say what we know and say no to what we do not. Only with such an honest attitude could we acquire true knowledge."

The popular saying we have now "Taking what is known as known, and what is unknown as unknown" had come from this. It has set a demand on us that we need to be honest in studies and free from even the slightest falsehood. We need to be good at learning and discovering new things. Though as young as kids, their questions arise from new perspectives and are different from adults, who might take them for granted. The kids cannot provide us answers; nevertheless they provide us food for thought.

37. 近朱赤，近墨黑

有一次，孔子与曾参谈起自己的几个学生，他断言："我死了之后，卜商的学识会不断增长，而端木赐则会一天不如一天。"曾参觉得很奇怪："您为什么这么说呢？"孔子说："你看，卜商喜欢和比自己贤能的人在一起，而端木赐却喜欢和不如自己的人在一起。你如果不知道某个人的儿子怎样，就看看做父亲的怎样；不知道某个人怎样，就看看他结交的朋友怎样；不知道君王怎样，就看看他所委任的臣子怎样；不知道某个地方怎样，就看看那个地方的草木植被怎样。所以有老话说，跟好人相处，就像进入充满芝兰香味的房子，时间长了就闻不出香味了，因为已经被芝兰的香味同化了。跟不好的人相处，就像进入卖咸鱼的店铺，时间长了，也闻不出臭味了，因为也已经被咸鱼的味道同化了。存放丹这种东西的地方往往是红色的，而存放漆这种东西的地方却往往是黑色的，所以一个君子一定要慎重地选择自己所处的环境。”

后世所说的“近朱者赤，近墨者黑”，表达了同样的意思。当年孟子的母亲为了儿子的健康成长，搬了三次家。选择一个有利于孩子学习生活的环境对孩子一生都是至关重要的。在明代洪自诚的名著《菜根谭》中也讲到，教导孩子就要跟养育女孩子一样谨慎，要严格管束他们的出入和所交往的朋友。万一不小心结交了坏人就等于在好好的地里种下了坏种子，长不出好禾苗来，这个孩子的一生也就毁了。别的不说，就看看那些染上吸毒恶习的人，如果没有接触的机会，怎会坠入万劫不复的深渊？

ONE TAKES THE COLOR OF ONE'S COMPANY

Confucius was once talking with Zeng Shen about his disciples. He said affirmatively, “After my death, Bu Shang will continue to gain in his knowledge, but Duanmu Ci will go the opposite way.”

Puzzled, Zeng Shen asked, “Why do you think so?”

Confucius told him, “Don't you see? Bu Shang always enjoys his company of the wiser, while Duanmu Ci stays with the inferior. From the father you see his son. From one's friend you see that person. From the ministers you see the duke. From the grass and woods you see the visage of a place. There is the old saying: it's like staying in a room with fragrant orchids when you stay with good people, you do not smell the fragrance as the smell in the room is already assimilated by the sweet orchids. Likewise, it's like staying in a salted fish stop when you stay with bad people, you do not smell the odor as the smell in the room is already assimilated by the fish. A container for vermilion is always red and that for lacquer is always dark. Therefore, a gentleman needs to be cautious in choosing his environment.

A saying of later times echoed that, "One takes the color of one's company." Mencius' mother moved three times only to find a good environment for his son, for a good environment played a crucial role for his son's studies. In *Zen of Vegetable Roots* (Cai Gen Tan) wrote by Hong Zicheng of the Ming Dynasty, it also states that the education of children needs to be cautious and special attention should be paid to their conducts and friends. If in case they have made vicious friends, their whole life would be ruined. It's like planting bad seeds in the field and no good seedlings can be expected. Take the drug addicts for example: how could they fall into such an abyss beyond redemption if they had no chances of having the drugs?

38. 无功不受禄

孔子的学生曾子，穿着破旧的衣裳耕田种地，鲁国国君派人前去赐予他食邑，并说："请用这个食邑的收入添置些衣裳。"曾子不肯接受。使臣回去告诉国君，国君命令使臣再去曾子那儿要曾子接受食邑，曾子还是不接受。使臣说："您并不是在向别人索取，是人家自愿送给您的，您为什么不肯接受呢？"曾子说："我听说，接受他人的东西便会畏惧他人，给予他人东西便会傲视他人。即使国君赐给我食邑而且不傲视我，我又怎么能不畏惧呢？"终究还是不肯接受。孔子听到这件事后说："曾参的话，足以为他保全自己的气节人格了。"

孔子不仅提倡曾参的做法，自己也身体力行。有一次，孔子谒见齐景公，齐景公要将廪丘（今山东鄄城东北）这个地方送给孔子作为食邑。孔子坚决推辞不肯接受，回来后告诉弟子说："我听说君子根据功劳接受俸禄，今天我去给景公提了个建议，景公还没开始实施这个建议，就要赏赐给我廪丘这个地方，他也太不了解我了。”命令弟子赶紧套车，告辞离开。

孔子、曾子这师徒二人都没有在利益面前动摇自己的信念，坚守“不义富且贵，与我如浮云”的气节。俗话说“鸟为食亡，人为财死”，“拿人家的手短，吃人家的嘴软”，这是令人畏惧的，要知道：财富有了，人格没了，躯体活着，精神死了，这才是最可怕的。

RECEIVING NO UNMERITED REWARD

Confucius' disciple Zeng Zi wore shabby old clothes to plow and plant. The duke of Lu dispatched an envoy to grant him a fief, and informed him to buy some clothing with the earnings. Zeng Zi, however, declined the offer. The envoy returned to his duke with the report, but was sent back to Zeng Zi on the same mission. Zeng Zi declined again. The envoy said, "You are not asking for, but being given out of free will. Why don't you accept it?"

"I have heard," Zeng Zi told him, "that fear would grow in one's heart after receiving other's giving, and that contempt would grow after giving something out. Though the Duke confers the fief without contempt, how could fears not grow in my heart?" Eventually he did not accept the offer. After learning that, Confucius remarked, "What Zeng Zi has said would suffice to preserve his moral integrity."

Not only did Confucius advocate the practice of Zeng Zi, but also he followed it himself. Once Confucius was meeting Duke Jing of Qi, and was offered a fief in Linqiu (present northeastern Juan Cheng of Shandong Province). But Confucius declined resolutely. After taking his leave, Confucius told his disciples, "I have learned that a gentleman receives a reward according to his contributions. Today

I made a proposal to Duke Jing. He has not put it into practice yet but would grant me a fief. He just does not know me!" Confucius ordered his disciples to fix up the harness and took their leave.

Confucius and his disciple Zeng Zi cherished their unshakable faith, and clung to the moral standard of "wealth and position obtained by unrighteous means are to me, floating clouds." As the saying goes, "men die in pursuit of wealth and birds die in pursuit of food", or "gifts blind the eyes", it is a terrible situation when one acquires wealth but loses his moral integrity, and when one is alive physically but dead in spirit.

39. 端木赐赎奴

鲁国有法令规定，鲁国人在其他国家给人当奴隶，如果有人能用钱把这个奴隶赎回来，可以从国库中拿回赎金。孔子的学生子贡（端木赐），从别的国家赎回来一个当奴隶的鲁国人，回到鲁国后却推辞不去官府那里取回用掉的钱。孔子听说这件事后就说："端木赐错了。从今以后，鲁国人不会再去赎买奴隶了。"……子路救了一个落水的人，那人给他一头牛作为回报，子路接受了。孔子听说后又说："鲁国人一定会拯救落水的人了。"

在《淮南子·道应训》、《说苑·政理》中也记载了类似的事，但孔子把话说得更直白些，他说："端木赐错了。圣人做事，足可以影响、改变民风民俗，并作为准则被后人广泛效法，而不可以仅仅作为个人的行为，只想满足自己修身养性、端正品行的需要。"

孔子是深切地了解人心的。我们说"无功不受禄"，反过来我们就应当提倡“有功当受禄”，因为受禄是对一个人行为的肯定，这种肯定不管是精神层面的还是物质层面的，都将使有功劳的行为得以传颂，得以效仿，使得实行此类行为的人越来越多，受益的人也自然越来越多，取得的社会效益一定大大高于付出的成本。当然，从个人修养来说，子贡的不谋报酬是高尚的，但不可能很快成为社会的普遍模式。

DUANMU CI REDEEMING A SLAVE

In the State of Lu it was ordained that anyone could be refunded by the state treasury if redeeming a Lu slave from another state. Confucius' disciple Duanmu Ci, also known as Zi Gong, did redeem one from another state. After returning, however, he refused to claim his expenses from the local court. After learning that, Confucius remarked, "So wrong was Duanmu Ci! Henceforth, no one from Lu would like to redeem slaves." Another disciple Zi Lu saved one from drowning. In return, the man gave him a buffalo and Zi Lu accepted. After hearing that, Confucius also remarked, "Now people in Lu would reach out to help when someone falls into water."

Similar accounts also appear in the *Responses of the Way* in *Huai Nan Zi*, and the *Principles of Government* in the *Garden of Sayings*, in which, however, Confucius voiced his opinion in a more straight way. He said, "Duanmu Ci was wrong. Whatever a sage does could show an impact and even change a folk custom, and become modeled after by future generations. He should not have taken it merely as a personal conduct to satisfy his own needs of self-cultivation and moral integrity."

Obviously, Confucius had a deep understanding of the human thoughts. When we say "receiving no unmerited reward", we must also encourage "receiving a reward after making a merit". That one receives a reward is to affirm his conduct. Be it spiritual or material, such affirmation would take meritorious conducts to the lips of everyone and create followers. As a result, there would be more similar conducts, and more to benefit. The social benefits thereupon achieved would surely be dramatically higher than the costs paid. It is for sure that Zi Gong showed high moral standard without going for a reward. However, he could not make himself a popular model for conduct, and therefore made the public feel remotely separated from such conducts.

40. 谦受益，满招损

孔子参观祭祀鲁桓公的庙时，看到一个奇巧的器皿。孔子问看守鲁桓公庙的人说："这是什么器皿？"看守人说："这大概就是置放在座位右边的那种器皿。"孔子说："我听说放在座位右边的器皿很奇特，里面空的时候器皿是倾斜的，往里注水，水量适中的时候器皿就是正的，再继续注水直到水满了，器皿就翻倒了。"说完，孔子回头跟弟子说："往里注水，咱们来看看。"弟子舀了水往里面灌。果然，水量适中的时候就正了，水满了就翻倒了，水倒完了就倾斜了。孔子很感慨地叹息道："唉，哪有满了不翻倒的呢？"子路提出问题："那怎样才能保持盈满呢？总该有办法保持盈满吧。"孔子说："特别聪明有智慧的人，要让大家看起来觉得笨笨的，才能保持长久；立下天大的功劳的，要主动退让，才能保持长久；勇猛强大超过大众的，要显得怯弱害怕，才能保持长久；富有四海，就要显得谦逊礼让，才能保持长久。

这就是所说的谦卑、退让、自损的方法。”

这个放在座位右边的器皿，就是用作提醒警示的。它用事实来告诉座位上的主人，水没有会倾斜，水太满会翻倒，只有不多不少才会端正稳定。相传也是孔子编集的《尚书·大禹谟》中讲到的“满招损，谦受益，时乃天道”，与这个器皿告诉我们的是相同的道理。在一个人一无所有的时候，容易谦卑好学，会努力通过各种方法让自己进步，当他慢慢强大，学识地位财富都在不断上升，得到万人仰慕的时候，他如果还保持着当年两手空空时的谦卑之心，那么他还能继续发展；相反，如果他洋洋自得，那么他就像装满了水的那个奇特器皿，开始走下坡路。当然，这个并不是告诉你，为了保持平衡和端正，我们只需要半瓶子水就够了，因为子路提出的问题就是“怎样才能保持盈满”？

MODESTY BENEFITS, PRIDE HURTS

When Confucius was paying homage to the temple of Duke Huan of Lu, he saw an artful vessel and asked the keeper what it was.

The keeper told him, “That might be the vessel placed on the right side of the seat.”

Confucius said, “I have heard such is a very special vessel. When it is empty, it tilts. When it is filled with water to a certain level, it goes upright. But if keep filling in water until full, it overturns.”

When he finished, he turned to his disciples, saying, “Now shall we fill it with water for a test?” As his disciples followed what he said, it did work when the water was medium the vessel turned upright. When it was full, it overturned. With strong emotion, Confucius sighed, “Is there anything that does not overturn when it is full?”

"Then is there a way to keep it full?" Zi Lu asked, "Anyway, there must be a way to keep it full."

Confucius answered, "If one is extremely smart and wise, he must make himself look silly so as to go long. If one has outstanding valor and power, he must make himself look timid so as to go long. If one is wealthy, he must remain humble and modest so as to go long. These are the ways to remain humble and concessive."

Therefore, such a vessel put on the right side of the seat served as a warning. It always reminded its master on the seat with facts that the vessel could tilt without water and overturn when it's full. It stood upright only when the water remained just appropriate. The same argument appeared in the *Counsels of Great Yu* in the *Book of History*, which is believed to be compiled by Confucius, that "Pride hurts and modesty benefits — this is the way of Heaven."

When one owns nothing, he tends to be humble and industrious to achieve progress. As he advances with knowledge, wealth and popularity, he would move still further if he could remain the original modesty. Otherwise, he would run downhill like the filled-up vessel. Surely, this does not mean one needs only half filled so as to remain balanced and upright, for the question posed by Zi Lu was "How to keep it full?"

41. 乐山乐水

孔子总说“仁者乐山，智者乐水”，可到底为什么这么说，为什么不说“仁者乐水，智者乐山”呢？所以终于有一天，子张问老师：“仁者为什么喜欢山啊？”孔子回答说：“山啊，又高又大。”子张听了这话，更奇怪了，山么当然是高大的，否则还叫山？他又追问：“为什么又高又大就喜欢呢？”孔子接着回答：“山，生长着草木，鸟啊兽啊在草木间繁衍，另外还长着很多有用的东西。产出这么多有用的东西，而且无私地供给人们采用。云啊风啊也从山里生出，通向天也通向地，调和阴阳二气，形成雨露洒遍大地，万物因此得以生长，百姓因此得以哺育，这就是仁者喜欢山的道理。”

子贡问孔子：“君子看见大河就要去观看，这是为什么啊？”老师说：“君子常常认为水是有优秀品德的：水流向四方，十分无私，很有美德；水流到的地方万物能够生长，水流不到的地方什么都不能成活，就像仁德；水往低处流，再怎么弯曲回折都还是顽固地遵循这个原则，就像正义；前面是万丈深的山谷，它也毫不畏惧，就像我们说的勇敢；水浅的地方潺潺流淌，水深的地方不可测量，就像人的智慧；它看上去很柔弱，却能通过任何危险的地带，就像能明察所有；可以包容不清洁的东西进入它的内部，让这东西变得清清爽爽地出来，就像善的教化；用它来衡量地平，类似公正；装满容器不需要用盖去刮它也会很平，就像公平；不管怎么迂回曲折总是东西流淌，就像坚定的意志不会改变。所以，君子见到大河就要去观看。”

孔子的一番话让弟子们恍然大悟。可不是，敦厚的山就像仁者，无私地产出草木鸟兽、云雾雨露而不需要任何回报；奔腾的长江大河就像谦谦君子，既刚强又柔美，既公正又纯洁，以自身的美德启示民众。

在世界思想史上，把地理环境与人的风格、品性、特征联系起来，有许多人这么做的，其中法国思想家孟德斯鸠算是很有名的，后人说他是地理环境决定论者，其实孔子也是这样。与孟德斯鸠相比，孔子有两大不同，首先孔子早于孟德斯鸠十几个世纪；其次，孔子没有孟德斯鸠那么绝对。

THE JOYS COMPARABLE TO MOUNTAINS AND RIVERS

Confucius always said, "The wise find joys in water and the benevolent find joys in mountains." But why? Why was it not the opposite — the benevolent like water and the wise like mountains?

One day, Zi Zhang asked the Master, "Why do the benevolent love mountains?"

"The mountains," Confucius said, "are high and lofty."

That mountains are always high and lofty is a matter of fact. Even puzzled, Zi Zhang asked, "Why should the benevolent love the mountains just because they are high and lofty?"

"In the mountains," Confucius continued, "there are grass and trees, in which the birds and beasts grow. Many other things of use also grow for man to use, and for nothing in return. Clouds and winds also rise from the mountains into the heaven and the earth to unify the *Yin* and *Yang* energies of life. Then they turn into rain and dews to nourish all plants on the earth. Thus the people are fed. Such is the reason for the benevolent to love the mountains."

Then Zi Gong asked, "Why should a gentleman make a visit when there is a great river?"

"A gentleman," said the Master, "always sees the virtues of water. Water flows into all directions selflessly — that is true virtue. Wherever the water reaches, all plants grow. Wherever there is no water, nothing can survive — that is benevolence. Water flows downward however winding the passage is — that is a principle and like justice. It does not show any fear when there is a bottomless valley — that is courage. When the water is shallow, the stream purls; when the water is deep, it is fathomless — that is like man's wisdom. It looks soft and weak, but it goes through any perilous terrains — that is like seeing through everything. It contains anything not clean in itself, and makes it clean — that is like the process of moral education. If using water to measure the level of land, it's similar to the function of justice. When filling water into a container, you need not the lid to scrape off the unwanted and it remains plane — that is like fairness. It flows however winding the passage is — that is like the perseverance of willpower. Such are the reasons for a gentleman to visit a great river."

His disciples were enlightened by the lecture. Sure enough, the lofty mountains are like the benevolent. Selflessly they produce grass, woods, birds, fog, rain and dews. The surging rivers are like a modest gentleman — unyielding and soft, impartial and pure. They inspire the people with their own virtues.

There have been quite a few in the world history of ideology that relate geographical circumstances to man's style, quality, and features. The French ideologist Montesquieu has been one of the well known with his so-called environmental determinism. Likewise, Confucius had similar propositions, but well over a millennium before Montesquieu. Moreover, the ideas of Confucius do not feature the Montesquieu-style of going to extremes.

42. 孔子之死

孔子病了，子贡去看他。孔子拄着拐杖在门口踱步，看到子贡来，说：“赐，你为什么这么晚才来呢？”接着又叹了口气，轻轻地唱道：“巍峨的泰山崩坏了，高高的梁柱折断了，哲人就这样枯槁了！”边唱边流泪。子贡听着，也是满心悲凄。

歇了歇，孔子又对子贡说：“天下不行正道已经很久了，这世上也没有人来尊崇我的主张。夏朝人死了，棺木停放在东厢的台阶旁；周朝人死了，棺木停放在西厢的台阶旁；殷朝人死了，棺木停放在厅堂的两根大柱之间。昨天晚上，我梦见自己坐在两个大柱中间，接受别人的祭奠。我的祖先就是殷朝人啊。”

又过了七天，孔子便去世了。

一代伟人默默逝去，理想抱负都如东逝水未曾实现。然而，他说过的话，做过的事，却让两千多年来的后人一直咀嚼、回味，影响了整个中国甚至世界。有的人活着，但他已经死了；有的人死了，但他依然活着。

THE DEATH OF CONFUCIUS

Confucius fell ill and his disciple Zi Gong visited him. He was strolling about on his sticks when he saw Zi Gong coming his way. "Zi Gong, how come you are so late?" Confucius sighed and then chanted softly, with tears, "The towering Mount Tai collapses. The tall post rives. The sage now withers!" Hearing that, Zi Gong's heart was laden with grief.

After a pause, Confucius told Zi Gong, "It's been long that no one practices the virtuous Way under Heaven, and no one follows my propositions. After the death of someone in the Xia Dynasty, their coffins were set on the stairs in the eastern hall. After the death of someone in the Zhou Dynasty, their coffins were set on the stairs in the western hall. After the death of someone in the Shang Dynasty, their coffins were set between two major posts. Last night I dreamt myself sitting between two big posts to receive people's worship. My ancestors came from the Shang dynasty."

Seven more days had passed, and Confucius closed his eyes.

A great man of the time passed away quietly, leaving his ideals and ambitions in vain. What he had said and done, however, have been food for thought for people for over two millennia. His influence have reached the whole China and even the world. Some are living but are dead. Some are dead but still living.

43. 苛政猛于虎

有一天，孔子和学生们经过泰山脚下的时候，无意中听到一位妇人呜呜咽咽的哭声，听上去十分悲伤。听到这样悲切的哭声，孔子便让子路过去看一下，问问怎么回事。

子路循着哭声找到那位妇人，很和气地问她："您哭得这么凄惨，一定是有很深的痛苦，能不能告诉我是怎么回事，看我们是否能帮助你。"

妇人听子路这么说，打量了他几眼，觉得他是个善良之人，便一五一十地说了她的遭遇："我的命真是苦啊！以前我的公公是被老虎咬死的，后来我的丈夫又被老虎咬死，如今我的儿子，……这么年轻的一个孩子，前天又被老虎咬死了。家里的男人都死了，留下我一个人，我可怎么活下去啊！"

子路听她说完，回到孔子车旁，把情况跟孔子复述了一遍。孔子跟着子路又来到那位妇人跟前，非常同情并且恭敬地问她："这里的老虎这么凶猛可怕，你们为什么不搬家到别的地方去生活呢？"

妇人哭哭啼啼地说道："向北去齐国吧，那儿的官吏太凶狠；向南去鲁国吧，那儿的苛捐杂税太多，老百姓都交不起。只有在这个老虎出没的山沟里，没人来管我们，我们还能勉强活下去……"

妇人的话让孔子沉默不语，脸色阴沉。他觉得怎么安慰妇人都是虚的，妇人一家宁愿死于虎口，也不愿离开这个不被苛政统辖的山沟，他甚至觉得自己也愧对这妇人一家。

孔子一行渐渐走远了，妇人的哭声还隐隐约约地伴随着。孔子长叹一声，对弟子们说："年轻人，你们要记住啊，苛政猛于虎，苛政猛于虎啊！"

孔子后来特意跟学生们讨论了为政的问题。他告诫学生们，将来从政的时候，一定要记得施行德政，千万不要采用苛政。施行德政，就如群星围绕着北斗星一样，老百姓就会围绕在施政者周围。施行德政，不仅要取消苛捐杂税，而且要先用诗书礼乐来教化百姓，在有问题的时候才用刑法来纠正百姓，让他们知廉耻，不犯罪，心悦诚服而吃穿无忧，这样国家就会稳定而且繁荣。

孔子以后两千年的中国历史是否验证了孔子的这个绝苛政而倡德政的道理呢？

OPPRESSIVE GOVERNANCE IS MORE FEARSOME THAN A TIGER

Once when Confucius was passing near the foot of Mount Tai in a carriage, there was a woman weeping sadly. At that Confucius sent Zi Lu over to see what was going on.

Following the weeping, Zi Lu found the woman and inquired of her, saying, "From the sound of your weeping, it seems that you indeed have deep-felt pains. Would you tell me what is the matter and see if we could do something?

After sizing him up for a while, the woman felt Zi Lu was of the kind type. Then she told Zi Lu every detail, "My life is really miserable! My father-in-law died in a tiger's jaw. Later my husband died after being mauled by a tiger too. Now, my son… At such a young age, he also died from that. No men are left in my family. I'm left alone, but how can I survive?"

After hearing that, Zi Lu returned to Confucius' carriage and reported what he had heard. Confucius then followed Zi Lu to see the woman. Filled with sympathy and respect, Confucius asked her, "If the tigers here are so fearsome, why haven't your family moved away?"

Her eyes teeming with tears, the woman said, "If we move to Qi to the north, the officials there are too fierce. If we move to Lu to the south, there are too many taxes for anyone to bear. Only in this valley with many tigers would there be nobody coming to us. Thus we could have managed to make a living."

Confucius was caught in a silence at her words, his face overcast. But he felt any consoling would be meaningless. The woman would rather die in the tiger's jaws than leave the valley that was free of oppressive government. Confucius even felt ashamed to face the woman.

Confucius and his people went away while the woman's weeping was still faintly in their ears. Heaving a deep sigh, Confucius told his disciples, "Young men, you must bear this in mind: A harsh and oppressive government is even more ferocious and fearsome than a tiger, even a tiger!"

Later on, Confucius had a special discussion with his disciples on governance. He warned that they should not practice oppressive governance when taking an office. With benevolent governance, the people would gather around the ruler just like the stars around the Big Dipper. To practice benevolent governance, the ruler should first remove all the exorbitant taxes and levies, and educate the people with poetry, calligraphy, rites and music. Penalties were used only to rectify mistakes and help the people to cultivate their sense of honor and stay away from crimes. The people would be gladly convinced when they were well fed and clothed. In that way, a state could remain stable and prosperous.

How the long history of over two millennia after Confucius had validated his warnings to eliminate oppressive governance and promote virtuous ruling!

44. 孔子的一次外交大胜

孔子 51 岁的时候得到了在鲁国担任中都宰的机会，因为政绩斐然，很快就被提拔为司空，接着又被提拔为司寇，司寇是中国古代主刑狱之官。在孔子担任司寇的时候，大约公元前 500 年，齐鲁两国有过一次夹谷会盟，在这次会盟上，孔子为鲁国争得了一次外交上的重大胜利。

鲁国当时的实力不如齐国，也不如晋国，他只能巧妙地利用他们之间的矛盾来取得对自己有利的局面，从而维持国家的生存。那时齐国要与晋国争霸，就与鲁国议和了。但是眼看着孔子的为政方针深得民心，鲁国形势蒸蒸日上，齐国又开始担心鲁国过分强大威胁到自己。于是齐国派使者向鲁定公约定夹谷会盟，名为友好，实想借此设计打压鲁国。

刚刚当上司寇的孔子领命作为鲁定公的相礼参加盟会。对此，孔子作了认真的研究与准备。他建议鲁定公要派一支精干的卫队，因为自古以来，文武两方面都是相辅相成的，有文事要配武备，有武事要配文备。鲁定公听从了孔子的建议，选定了强有力的军官与卫兵。与此同时，齐国人知道对方派孔子作相礼，也在研究孔子。因为十多年前孔子曾经在齐国住过几年，虽然因为种种原因，齐景公没有任用孔子，但孔子的学养在齐国还是颇有影响。不过，齐臣犁弥认为孔子只是一个文人，柔弱胆怯无勇。如果派夹谷当地的莱人用武力劫持鲁侯，孔子一定没办法对付，不得不依从齐国的条件。

会盟的那天，齐侯由晏婴陪同，鲁侯由孔子陪同，来到夹谷。夹谷特地建了盟坛，排了席位，修了三级土台阶，鲁定公与齐景公相互作揖谦让登上盟坛。双方先是宴饮献酬，然后齐国的一个小官吏快步走近说："请演奏四方的乐舞。"齐景公点头赞同，于是莱人就挥着旗子，舞着羽毛，握着矛戟剑盾，敲着鼓呐喊着表演起来。一边表演，一边慢慢地向鲁定公靠近。

孔子看到这样的情况，果断地快步向前，一步跨上两个台阶，挥着长袖说："我们齐鲁两国的君主在这儿进行友好盟会，为什么让夷狄的乐舞到这儿来？这样做是违反礼仪的。请下令撤走。"齐景公感到心虚尴尬了，有些愧疚，而且发现孔子也不像预想的那样胆小怕事，听人摆布。所以，他只好挥手让莱人撤下去。

不多一会儿，齐国的小官吏又快步走近说："请演奏宫中的舞乐。"齐景公又同意了。一些侏儒艺人便嬉笑着上前表演。孔子见状，还是觉得不妙，立刻快步向前，一步跨上两个台阶，严厉地说："好的酒器不出宫门，好的音乐不在野外演奏。如果用低等的音乐而又侮辱君主，这些侏儒艺人胆敢蛊惑诸侯，应该诛杀！"自知失礼也失利的齐国方面，只好听从孔子的说法，杀了这些被利用的艺人。

齐景公内心受到震动，感到恐惧。他知道这次从理从礼来说都不如鲁国，回到齐国后，批评他的群臣："人家鲁国的臣子用君子之道来辅佐君主，而你们呢？用那些夷狄之道来教我，害得我得罪了鲁君。这下反倒弄巧成拙，怎么办？"有个机灵的官吏回答齐景公："君子有个过错就用实际行动来道歉，小人有了过错只用花言巧语来道歉。您若是真的觉得对此感到抱歉，而且恐惧，那就用实际行动去道歉吧。”于是，齐景公就按照孔子提出来的要求，把以前侵占的鲁国的三个地方的田地还给了鲁国，以示歉意。

在这次盟会中，孔子使鲁国在强齐面前赢得了体面，并且收回了失去的田地，立了大功！其实，孔子的这次胜利是幸运的。倘若齐国不把礼仪放在眼里，那么，孔子的言辞再激烈也保护不了鲁侯及鲁国的面子。所以，不讲礼仪不行，因为世界如果没有这些规则，整个地球都会毁灭在你死我活的争夺中；当然也不能夸大礼仪的作用，因为它的作用不是无限的。

A DIPLOMATIC TRIUMPH

At the age of 51, Confucius was appointed Officer-in-Charge of Zhongdu. For his achievements, he was soon elevated to be Director of Engineering, and later Minister of Justice in charge of penalty and prison. During his term as Minister of Justice, the states of Qi and Lu had a summit at Jiagu in approximately 500 BC. It was in that summit that Confucius achieved a significant diplomatic triumph.

At the time, the State of Lu was not as powerful as its neighboring states of Qi and Jin. What Lu could do was to count on its skills to take advantage of the conflicts between Qi and Jin to safeguard its existence. Meanwhile, should Qi intend to seek hegemony over Jin, it would have to make peace with Lu. As the practice of Confucius' policies won wide popularity and the State of Lu was thriving, the State of Qi worried the threat from a strong State of Lu. Thus Qi appointed special envoys to invite Duke Ding of Lu for a summit at Jiagu to inhibit Lu though in the name of friendship.

As the newly appointed Minister of Justice, Confucius was made the Master of Ceremonies for Duke Ding of Lu at the summit. After thorough studies and preparations, Confucius advised his duke to take a brigade of strong escorts. He stated that from ancient times, civil and military affairs had been supplementing each other. Meanwhile, the Qi rulers were studying Confucius as they knew his role in the summit. Over a decade ago, Confucius had lived for a few years in Qi, but he did not receive any serious attention from Duke Jing for many reasons. However, Confucius' doctrines did have exerted some influence in Qi. While the Qi minister Li Mi regarded Confucius as merely a man of letters without much valor. Therefore, Qi would be at ease in getting Lu to submit if they could get local *Lai* warriors to hijack the duke of Lu.

On the day of the summit in Jiagu, the duke of Qi was escorted by Yan Ying and the duke of Lu by Confucius. Seats having been well lined, a special alliance altar with three flights of steps was already set. Bowing with folded hands, the two dukes observed the conventional rites and ascended the altar. They started with a banquet, offering each other their appreciation. Then a junior officer moved forward and requested to the duke of Qi, saying, "Your Majesty, may we play the Four Direction Music Dance?" Duke Jing nodded his consent. So some *Lai* men waved flags and feathers with shafts, swords and shields in hands, beating drums amongst hilarious cheers. As the performance was going on, the *Lai* men moved slowly toward Duke Ding.

Seeing that, Confucius trotted ahead decidedly, two stairs at a step. Waving his long sleeves, Confucius cried out, "It is the dukes of Qi and Lu meeting here today. But what is the point to get such foreign music dances? This surely goes against the rites. May I request that they be removed?" Rather awkward and guilty, Duke Jing realized that Confucius was not a coward for anyone to manipulate. Thus he had to wave out the *Lai* men.

In a short while, the junior officer of Qi showed up again, saying, "Your

Majesty, may we play the palace dancing music now?" Duke Jing nodded his approval. Then a band of dwarf players moved forward. Confucius felt it suspicious and trotted ahead again, two stairs at a step. In a rather rigorous tone, he said, "A fine drinking vessel is not carried out of the palace gates. A fine music is not played in the wild outdoors. Now these dwarfs are playing such lowly music to insult our dukes. They deserve immediate execution!" Losing their ground in etiquette, the Qi side had to follow the suggestion made by Confucius, and killed the dwarf players.

Duke Jing of Qi felt shocked and frightened, as he knew well Qi had not gained anything in either the argument or the rites against Lu. After return, he criticized his ministers, "Now, you see! The ministers of Lu assisted their duke in a virtuous Way. What are the good of you except suggesting the foreign tricks? What you took as smart tactics is now merely foolish stuff, and I have offended the duke of Lu. Now you advise me on the next step!" A shrewd official in the court came up with an idea, saying, "A gentleman mends up his way through specific moves. A petty man mends up his way with specious talk. Should Your Majesty feel sorry and fearful for it, then it would be advisable that you take actual actions." Therefore, as a way to express his regrets, Duke Jing of Qi returned the three captured lands to the State of Lu according to Confucius' requirements.

In the summit, Confucius had rendered a meritorious service by winning grace for Lu in face of the powerful Qi and resuming the lost lands of Lu. Actually, Confucius was lucky. However vehement his rhetoric might be, Confucius would be incapable to safeguard the grace of either the duke or the state if Qi disregarded rites. However, our world would not do without rites as that would surely lead our globe to deadly fights. Though it stands to no reason to magnify the function of rites, nevertheless rites do have their limited effects.

45. 堕三都之败

在齐鲁边境有三个城邑：郈邑、费邑和成邑。它们分别属于叔孙氏、季孙氏和孟孙氏，也就是鲁国的三桓。这三个城邑是鲁公封赏给三桓的，以奖励他们的辅政之功，也让他们三人因为自己的封邑而尽心保卫鲁国的边疆。然而鲁公没想到的是，这三桓慢慢地将这三邑建得越来越大，筑高了城墙又在城内囤积了大量的粮草，以致于能跟国君鲁公对抗，使得三桓在鲁国的权势和地位实际上已经高过了鲁公。人们就将这三个城邑称为“都”，习惯上就叫“三都”。

不过，就像三桓实际上掌控了鲁公一样，这三桓的家臣们居然也渐渐地掌握了这三都的管理权，成了三都的事实代言人，甚至能进一步操纵鲁国。他们也同样是把这三都作为根据地的，让三都的三个主人非常狼狈。有一年，侯犯以郈邑作为据点叛变叔孙氏，并与齐人联系，打算跟齐人作交换，把郈邑给齐人，自己在齐国得到一块土地，便于保住自己的利益。虽然这个侯犯的叛变被挫败，齐人后来也把郈还给了鲁，但这件事让三桓认识到这三都已经成为家臣的地盘，形势非常不妙。

怎么办？

当时子路在季孙氏那儿做事。孔子与子路共同谋划，试图拆除城邑，这样既削弱了三桓的家臣，同时也减弱了三桓的势力，从而使得鲁公的权势得以保证。这样也就合周礼的规定：家中不能藏有盔甲武器，作为封邑的城也不可以建高大的城墙。没有了这三个大都，也就不会再有家臣叛变的可能。

因为叔孙氏的郈邑已经被侯犯拿去跟齐人换了齐国的一个城邑，虽然齐人后来又还给了鲁，但侯犯已经逃亡，没有人掌控郈邑了，拆毁郈邑就很容易。第一个“都”很顺利就拆了。

季孙氏的费邑当时由公山弗狃控制着，自然不会轻易拱手相让。他组织了一帮人马先发制人去进攻鲁城，并且很快就攻入城中，使得鲁公与三桓都逃到了季孙氏的武子之台去躲着。公山还不罢休，继续进攻武子之台。孔子命令大将带兵拼死与公山的部队作战，打败了公山的人马。他们逃亡齐国，孔子等便把第二个“都”费邑也拆了。

最后一个“都”是孟孙氏的成邑。掌管成邑的是公敛处父，他对主人孟孙氏比较忠诚。孟孙氏和公敛处父之间也没什么大的矛盾。孟孙氏只不过是碍于面子才跟着叫几声“堕都”，其实他并不想真的堕了自己的城邑。公敛也是个聪明人，他跟孟孙氏说，成邑很重要，是鲁国北边的屏障，要是成邑拆了，那么齐人就很容易打到鲁国的北门。再说了，成邑是孟孙氏的保障，拆了成邑，也就毁了孟氏。孟孙氏自然听从了公敛的意见，由公敛守城，坚决不让孔子的人攻进去。而季孙氏和叔孙氏从自己的利益考虑，知道巩固了鲁公的权力，也就没有自己的势力了。因此慢慢地离开了孔子的统一战线，不参与堕城。孔子没办法攻下成邑，双方对峙了很久，只好不了了之。

孔子堕三都之败，根本原因在于孔子的目标与三桓的目标并不一致。孔子是为了维护周礼，重整君君臣臣的秩序；而三桓却只想解决家臣犯上的问题。所以，当孔子堕三都的计划触及三桓的利益时，矛头从家臣转到了三桓的时候，孔子就失去了鲁国的实权人物三桓的支持，计划自然失败。

DEFEAT IN ELIMINATING THE POWER OF THREE FIEFS

Along the border between Qi and Lu, there were three fief cities — Hou, Fei, and Cheng ruled by three clans (or *Huan* as they were called), Shu Sun, Ji Sun and Meng Sun respectively. The duke of Lu had conferred the fiefs to the three *Huan* for their contributions in assisting the governance of the dukedom, and as an incentive for them to protect the borders. However, Duke Lu had never anticipated that the three *Huan* gradually expanded their fiefs, strengthened their city walls, and housed huge stock of grains in such a way that they could defy the duke of the state. The three *Huan* had virtually outdone Duke Lu in power and status. The three cities were generally identified as capitals, and collectively they were called "trio-capitals".

However, just like the three *Huan* that were holding Duke Lu in their control, the retainers in the three *Huan* clans gradually secured the actual powers, and became their de facto representatives. They could even exert their influence on the whole state. As these ministers were taking their respective cities as their power base, the three nominal owners were caught in a wretched plight. One year, Hou Fan in the city of Hou launched a coup d'état against Shu Sun. He plotted with the State of Qi that he would trade Hou with a piece of a land in Qi in order to safeguard his interests. Though the coup d'état was smashed and the State of Qi returned Hou to the State of Lu, the incident led all the three *Huan* to a consensus that their cities had already become the sphere of influence of the ministers. It was a situation of anything but reassuring.

What to do then?

Meanwhile, Zi Lu was working for Ji Sun. In order to safeguard the power of Duke Lu, Confucius planned with Zi Lu to remove the three cities in a way to cripple the powers of the ministers and the three *Huan* as well. They quoted the old doctrine of Zhou rites: no military force in a dignitary family and no fief township should have high city walls. With the power of these three eliminated, there would be no chance for future clan coup d'état.

Shu Sun's city of Hou had already been traded off to the State of Qi by Hou Fan who got a city in Qi, but Hou was later on returned to Lu. Hou Fan had escaped and now there was a power vacuum in the city. Thus it was rather easy for Confucius to accomplish the mission.

The city Fei owned by Ji Sun was under the control of Gongshan Foniu, who would not easily give up. Preemptively, however, Gongshan Funiu dispatched a brigade to attack the dukedom capital, forcing Duke Lu and the three *Huan* to flee to the Wu Zi Altar owned by Ji Sun. Not ready to stop, Gongshan continued attacking the altar. Confucius ordered his generals to wage a desperate fight against the Gongshan troops. Eventually the Gongshan troops were defeated and they escaped to the State of Qi. Confucius then had the second city removed.

The last of the mission was Meng Sun's city Cheng, which was under control of Gonglian Chufu. Rather loyal to his master, Gonglian Chufu did not have any serious conflicts with Meng Sun. Meng Sun shouted the slogan of "removing the cities" merely for the sake of etiquette, though in fact he did not intend to see his own city to be removed. Wise enough as he was, Gonglian advised Meng Sun to note the importance of the city of Cheng as it was the northern defense for the State of Lu. If Cheng was removed, the State of Qi would find it easy to attack the north part of Lu. Furthermore, as the city of Cheng was the stronghold of Meng Sun, the removal of Cheng would be equal to put an end to

Meng Sun clan. Surely Meng Sun followed the advice of Gonglian, and had him defend the city against Confucius' troops. Meanwhile, both Ji Sun and Shu Sun knew the consolidation of Duke Lu's power would mean the loss of their own, and by and by they dumped Confucius' united front to remove the cities. Unable to capture Cheng after long confrontation of the two sides, Confucius had to wrap up his mission unaccomplished.

Fundamentally, Confucius' defeat in removing the three cities lied in the fact that his goal did not overlap that of the three *Huan*. For Confucius, he aimed to restore the ancient Zhou rites and the order between the ruler and the ministers. The three *Huan*, however, had their mind only on their offensive retainers. Therefore, when his plan started to erode the interests of the three *Huan*, the stake turned from the offensive ministers to their owners. Thus naturally, Confucius' plan suffered crushing defeat when he lost the support from the three *Huan*, the actual power holders.

46. 哀弟子颜渊之死

孔子带着弟子在外奔波了十多年，68 岁才回到鲁国。然而回到鲁国便接二连三地遭受打击。先是夫人亓官氏去世，一年后儿子孔鲤也先孔子而亡。又过了两年，孔子最心爱的弟子颜渊也病倒了。孔子天天派年轻的弟子去颜渊家探问、安慰，并给予必要的帮助。可是，老师和同窗的温暖与关心并没能挽回颜渊的生命，颜渊得病不久就命丧黄泉。

孔子得知，痛心疾首，宛如五雷轰顶。他捶着自己的胸脯哭喊："老天啊，你真是要了我的命啊!老天啊，你真是要了我的命啊！"哭了许久还是停不下来。弟子们劝慰他，让他节哀，以免悲伤过度。孔子反问弟子："我难道悲哀过度了吗？我不为颜渊这样的人悲伤，还为谁悲伤呢？"对于颜渊之死，孔子的伤心胜过自己儿子孔鲤的离世。颜渊是孔子最为看重，期望将来能继承自己衣钵的弟子，不仅聪明，有极好的悟性，而且具有高尚的道德，不迁怒，不贰过，三月不违仁。这位弟子之死，给孔子的打击是巨大的，大家都觉得孔子因此一下子老了不少。

颜渊的父亲颜无繇是个穷人，家里勉强给颜渊做了口棺材，却没钱置办外棺——椁。老父觉得这样对待儿子太简陋了，让儿子很不体面，便去求孔子，希望孔子能替颜渊买椁。

颜渊追随孔子多年，没有出仕为官，没有挣过一点儿钱。他父亲的这种想法也是可以理解的。可是孔子的回答让颜渊的老父十分意外，他说："无繇啊，丧事不能马虎，但也不能超过自己的承受能力。要根据家里的情况来定，即便是有钱人也不能逾越礼仪。既然没钱，就不妨装敛下葬就可以了。我儿子孔鲤下葬时也没有椁啊。"颜渊的老父还是不甘心，他认为自己的儿子在孔门弟子中是有特殊地位的，理应有椁。他知道孔子有辆车，恳求孔子把车卖了，换个椁回来给颜渊。

孔子还是摇头拒绝了："无繇啊，你怎么会不懂得我的意思呢？不是我舍不得卖车，而是卖车买椁是违背礼仪的。我没有什么实际的职务，但怎么说也是个大夫，按照规矩，大夫出门不能徒步而行，没有车我就不守礼了。而这样给颜渊买椁，对颜渊而言，也是不守礼。这样多不好！颜渊要是知道了，肯定不会同意的。"

孔子要坚决按照礼制来做，尽管他心里也想厚葬颜渊。孔子的另外一些弟子，也是特别敬重颜渊，他们也是不忍心颜渊就一口薄棺材下葬。于是，大家凑了钱，买了椁，葬了颜渊。孔子得知，内心复杂。一方面，他觉得这样违了礼，简直是对颜渊的不尊重；另一方面又觉得最心爱的弟子得以很好地下葬，对活着的自己、颜渊的老父及其他弟子们都是个安慰。所以，他也没有责怪那几个弟子，而像颜渊活着时那样对颜渊说："回啊，你一直把我当父亲看，可我却没能把你当儿子一样看。孔鲤死的时候，他的葬礼没有违礼，你的葬礼却违了礼。唉，你的同学们也是好意，不是我的主意啊。"

孔子是克己奉礼的圣人，孔子也是个充满情感、有着常人心肠的凡人。他的哀伤、他的克制、他的宽慰，让我们看到了一个用严格的原则来强烈抑制自己柔和亲情的老人，看到了一个血肉丰满的老人。

GRIEF OVER THE DEATH OF HIS DISCIPLE YAN YUAN

After running about for over a decade with his disciples, Confucius had not returned to his home State of Lu until age 68 only to suffer blows one after another. His wife Lady Qiguan passed away. One year later, his son Kong Li died. Barely two years had passed before his most favorite disciple Yan Yuan fell ill. Confucius sent his younger disciples to visit him, and offered necessary help. However, the warmth and care from Confucius and his disciples could not detain Yan Yuan's life, and he died soon.

Confucius became deeply saddened at Yan Yuan's death, and wailed without restraint, "Heaven, you have bereft me! Heaven, you have bereft me!" Confucius was in such a grief that he could not stop wailing. His disciples tried to make Confucius restrain his grief. "Should I restrain my grief?" Confucius asked them, "If I do not lament over people like Yan Yuan, then over whom?"

The grief Confucius had over the death of Yan Yuan exceeded that for his own son Kong Li. Having valued Yan Yuan so much, Confucius had hoped him to inherit his mantle. Yan Yuan was not only smart with outstanding apprehension but with a noble and virtuous mind. He would never vent his anger on others or repeat his mistakes. For three months there would be nothing in his mind contrary to perfect virtue. The death of such a disciple was a huge blow on Confucius, making the old age even more apparent on him.

Yan Yuan's father Yan Wuyao had been living in destitution. The Yan family barely made the inner coffin for him, but could not afford the outer part any more. The old father felt it was too mean for his decent son, and went to Confucius for assistance. He wished Confucius would buy his son the outer coffin.

Having followed Confucius for years, Yan Yuan, however, had never taken any public service or earned a single penny. His father's action was obviously understandable. Whereas Confucius' response was beyond the old man's expectation: "Wuyao, you should be serious on the funeral, but you need also keep it within your capacity. The funeral should be in accordance with your family condition. Even rich people should not exceed the limits of rites. Now since you are poor, why not just set the coffin and have him buried? My son Kong Li did not have an outer coffin either." Not reconciled, the old father still held a belief that his son deserved an outer coffin, for he knew his son had a special status among Confucius' disciples. He knew Confucius had a carriage, and pled him to trade it off for a coffin for Yan Yuan.

Shaking his head, Confucius declined, saying, "Wuyao, you haven't got my point! It is not that I hate to give up my carriage, but that I would violate the rites if I trade it off. Though I hold no real position, I'm in any case a *Dafu* in name. A *Dafu* need taking a carriage instead of on foot when going out, otherwise it's against the rites. Now if I trade off my carriage for Yan Yuan's coffin, it would be going against rites as well. That's rather bad. Yan Yuan would not favor it should he know."

Confucius insisted to follow the rites, though he had hoped to hold an elaborate funeral for Yan Yuan. Some of his disciples could not have the heart to see Yan Yuan go with a simple coffin and out of their respect they pooled their money to buy a coffin for Yan Yuan. Confucius had mixed feelings after learning that. On the one hand, he felt it was against the rites. While on the other, a decent burial for his disciple was a good comfort for himself, the old father and his other disciples. Therefore, he did not blame his disciples, but just talked to Yan Yuan as if he were alive, "Yan Yuan, you had taken me as your father, but I could not treat you as my son. When Kong Li died, his funeral did not violate the rites. But now yours did. It was, however, the good intention of your fellows, not mine!"

Confucius was a sage who denied himself and followed the rites. Meanwhile, he was also a person with affections and the heart of common people. With his sorrows, self-control, and comfort, a vivid image with blood and flesh of an old man, who restrained his affections with stiff principles, stands right before us.

47. 孔子为什么赦免了打官司的父子俩

孔子担任鲁国大司寇期间，有一对父子来打官司，两人谁也不让谁。孔子便把两人都抓起来，关在同一间牢房里，不审不问，关了三个月也没判决。终于有一天，那个做父亲的受不了了，提出了撤诉。孔子立刻叫人把父子俩都赦免了。

鲁国的掌权人物季孙氏听说后，很是不高兴，认为孔子骗了他。他说："以前司寇告诉我，治理一个国家一定要把孝道放在首位。现在我想惩罚一个不孝之人来教育百姓，难道不好吗？司寇怎么又赦免了他们呢？"冉有把季孙氏的这番话告诉了孔子。

孔子长长地叹息了一声，说道："唉，如果是在上位的人失去道义，却诛杀位居其下的人，这合理吗？教育百姓不用孝道，却用刑戮，这不是滥杀无辜吗？军队打了败仗，总不能把士兵都统统杀掉吧？监狱管理得不好，不能再惩罚犯人。"孔子顿了顿，脸上的神色更严峻了，沉默了一下，他继续说道："为什么这么说呢？在上位的人不先推行措施来教化百姓，百姓有了过错，罪责也不在百姓。不教化而直接推行命令进行严厉的诛罚，这是对百姓的残害；征收赋税苛刻而繁多，这是对百姓的残暴；不给尝试的机会便要求成功，这是对百姓的虐待。为政的人要杜绝这三种情况后，才可以考虑施用刑罚。"

孔子看冉有认真地听着，就问他，"你记得《书》上说的'要施行正义的刑罚、正义的诛杀，不要让刑罚和诛杀来迁就自己的想法，应该总是反思是自己还没有把事情办顺利、办妥当'。这句话的真正意思是什么？"冉有想了想，问，"是不是就是说'必须推行教化，然后才能施用刑罚'？"

孔子点点头，"是啊。要先陈述道德的教育，并且自己首先身体力行；如果不行，再通过受人尊崇的贤人来劝勉百姓；如果还不行，就把没有才能的官员撤换了；这样还行不通，就只能用威严的命令来震慑那些不道德的百姓。如此这番进行三年的教育，百姓就会都走上正途了。万一还有邪恶的人不听从教化，那么只能用刑罚来进行处置。这样的措施，才会让百姓都知道什么是犯罪。这样，那些刑罚只需要设置，基本上不需要使用。"

说到这儿，孔子问冉有，"你看看现在是什么情况，是不是像《诗》上说的'朝廷有重要的大臣辅佐天子，可以使百姓心里没有迷惑'？"没等冉有回答，他自己摇摇头，继续说道："现在完全不是这样啊。各种教令混乱无序，刑罚繁重，使百姓迷惑不解，无所适从，反而导致犯罪。百姓一犯罪，就用刑罚来惩戒，导致刑罚越来越重，而各种坏事还是层出不穷。"

孔子指了指不远处的门槛，说："假设这门槛三尺高，那即便是空车也拉不过去，为什么？因为门槛是直立陡峭的。而百仞(一仞为七尺或八尺)的高山，却连装载着重物的车也能拉上去，为什么？因为有缓缓倾斜的山坡。当今的社会，就像这有着斜坡的高山，即使制定了刑法，百姓也能越过去。"

孔子的教化思想自然是有很多问题的。但孔子所阐述的教育与刑法对百姓所起的作用却是清晰明确的。直到今天，我们也应该只是把刑法看做戒尺放在一边作为警示，而不是随时随地操起戒尺来乱打一气。教育是所有政府首先要考虑的重大问题，对教育方法的探讨是重中之重。

WHY PARDON THE FATHER AND HIS SON?

While serving as the Minister of Justice in the State of Lu, Confucius once had a father and his son in the court. The two accused each other, neither would give in. Thus Confucius put them both into one same cell for three months, bringing them to no trials or verdict. Eventually, the father could bear no longer and requested to withdraw. Confucius had both the father and his son released right away.

The case came to the ears of Ji Sun, a leading man in power in Lu. He was very unhappy, and took it that Confucius had played double, commenting, "I had heard from the Minister we should put filial piety on the first place in governing a state. But now, would we better punish a disobedient son to educate the people? If so, why had the Minist r pardoned them?" Ran You passed on the talk to Confucius.

Heaving a deep sigh, Confucius said, "Well, would it be justified for a ruler who does not follow the Way and execute one under his rule? Resorting to death penalty rather than filial piety is to murder the innocent. Can we execute all the soldiers just because the army is defeated? Now as our prison is not well managed, we cannot get the inmates answerable." With a pause and a grimmer face, Confucius continued, "Why so? Should the rulers take no measures to educate the people, they could not hold the people accountable for their misconducts. To enforce severe penalties directly without education is cruel harm to the people. To levy heavy and various taxes is atrocity to the people. To demand success without giving chances to try is to abuse the people. For rulers, they should make sure to eliminate all these three before resorting to penalties."

Seeing Ran You so attentive, Confucius asked, "In the *Book of History*, it reads, 'To practice justified penalties and killing and never yield to one's subjective thoughts. Always bear in mind to reflect whether the things have been handled properly.' Now, do you understand its true meaning?" Pondering for a moment, Ran You asked, "Does it mean we should 'render moral education before resorting to physical penalties'?"

Nodding in agreement, Confucius said, "Yes, moral education should be where we start with, and practice it ourselves. If that does not work, we need educate people through the well-respected sages. If that does not work, we need dismiss the incompetent officials. If that does not work, we need resort to severe decrees to hold the immoral ones in awe. As such, the commoners would get on to the right track in a matter of three years. In case there still are evil ones that defy the education, we can only resort to penalties. That way, the people will understand what a crime is, and eventually, the penalties will be more a need on paper than in practice."

Confucius turned to Ran You, asking, "Now, in the *Book of Odes*, it reads, 'In the court there is the virtuous to assist the King. And we the people would have nothing to confuse.' Do you feel we are in a time as depicted?" Before Ran You could open his mouth, Confucius shook his head and continued, "No! Now the decrees are in disorder, and the penalties are too severe. Thus the people feel confused and know not what to follow. That merely leads to crimes. The crimes then lead to penalties, and in turn, the penalties get increasingly severe, and crimes emerge one after another."

Pointing to the threshold nearby, Confucius said, "Were this threshold three feet high, a carriage though vacant could not be pulled over. Why? The threshold is vertical and steep. Now for a several hundred feet high mountain, a fully loaded carriage could be pulled up. Why? There is a slope. Our society is just like a mountain with a slope. Despite the mountain of penal codes, people could still climb it over."

Obviously, there are quite a few defects in Confucius' views on moral education. His propositions on the function of education and penalty on the people, however, still show their explicit worth. Even now, we can only take criminal laws as a sword of Damocles for the sake of warning, rather than wielding the sword ad libitum. Education should be of primary concern for all governments, and more importantly, specific means of education should be a top priority.

48. 预料子路之死

子路在卫国执政大臣孔悝家做家臣——邑宰，对孔悝忠心耿耿。前480年(鲁哀公15年)，卫国出公与父亲蒯聩争夺王位的斗争有了新的发展。因为蒯聩的姐姐，也就是孔悝的母亲伯姬在丈夫去世后与仆人浑良夫私通，而浑良夫又不是个能为爱而舍命的人，担心情事暴露会被杀头问罪。这桩情事恰好被蒯聩知道了，蒯聩便想利用浑良夫的忐忑不安来谋得王位，取代出公。蒯聩威逼利诱浑良夫，他对浑良夫许诺，只要浑良夫帮助他得到王位，他便免浑良夫三次死罪，并且还封他大夫的职衔。浑良夫和伯姬一商量，认为既然蒯聩能帮他俩做长久夫妻，不如就答应了蒯聩的要求，帮助蒯聩胁迫孔悝，让孔悝支持蒯聩称王。

那年的闰十二月，蒯聩偷偷地从戚邑来到孔伯姬家里，由姐姐伯姬领着去找外甥孔悝，拿长枪逼着孔悝，要孔悝与他们盟誓为伍，然后又押着孔悝登上孔家的高台，让卫出公知道孔悝已经倒向蒯聩一边。卫出公得知孔悝已经被蒯聩掌握，只好带着一部分人逃到鲁国去。

忠诚憨厚的子路听说自己的主人孔悝被胁持，不顾一切赶去救援。路上遇到孔子另一个在卫国作大夫的弟子子羔。子羔劝阻他，“你也不必管政事，快走吧，别去白白送死！”子路却慷慨激昂地说：“我是吃孔家饭的人，我不能丢下主人不管，只顾自己逃命。”还是坚决地冲到孔家高台，冲着高台大喊：“太子你何必扣留孔悝！即使杀了孔悝，还会有别人来阻止你上台的！你这个胆小鬼，我要烧高台了，等我把台子烧掉一半，看你放不放孔悝！”蒯聩听了这些话，气得要死，派了勇猛的武士到台下去杀子路。子路寡不敌众，斗了几个回合后被刺中要害，倒在血泊里。奄奄一息的子路缓缓地坐起来，理理头发，把头盔戴好，结好帽缨说，“君子死了，帽子也不能歪斜着。”众人被子路的举动惊呆了，看着子路艰难地整理好头盔战袍，无怨无悔地离去。

孔子在鲁国听说卫国的事变时，自然地想到了子羔和子路这两个在卫国任职的弟子，为此忧心忡忡。他寝食不安，总是念叨：“柴也其来，由也死矣！”

了解弟子的莫过于孔子了。他熟悉每位弟子的个性：子羔不会干预或者参与到事变中，他多半会逃回到鲁国；而子路，虽然常常呈“暴虎冯河，匹夫之勇”，却也总是牢记“临危不惧，见义勇为”之训，他为人最讲忠和义，必定不会丢下孔悝自己逃生，所以多半性命难保。几天后，孔子的预料完全得到了验证，子羔回来了，而子路的死讯也送到了。

孔子放声痛哭，吩咐弟子们在中庭祭奠子路。听说子路死后还被剁成肉酱，更是悲伤难忍。老年丧子，又接连失去心爱的弟子，白发人送黑发人，孔子的心情可想而知。

此后数月，孔子病倒。又过不久，孔子辞世。也许，孔子在预料子路的死时，也已经预料到自己时日无多。

ANTICIPATING THE DEATH OF ZI LU

As a magistrate, Zi Lu remained loyal to Kong Kui who was then a senior minister in the court of Wei. In year 480 BC in the State of Wei, Duke Chu's fight for throne with his father Kuai Kui escalated. Kong Kui's mother Boji, also Kuai Kui's sister, had an illicit love with a servant named Hun Liangfu after her husband passed away. However, Hun Liangfu was not one that could sacrifice his life for love, and was rather apprehensive to be exposed as that would lead to death penalty. It so happened that Kuai Kui learned of the scandal and then schemed to make use of Hun Liangfu. With threats and inducements of death pardon thrice and a senior position, Kuai Kui tried to secure Hun Liangfu's assistance. After consulting with Boji, Hun Liangfu thought he should take advantage of Kuai's promise to stay with her. To achieve that, he would assist in threatening Kong Kui to secure the throne for Kuai Kui.

It was a leap month of December when Kuai Kui sneaked from Qi Yi to Kong Boji's house. Kuai Kui followed his sister Boji to meet his nephew Kong Kui. With a long shaft in hand, he forced Kong Kui to swear his assistance. Then they escorted Kong Kui to the high clan altar to show Duke Chu that Kong Kui had turned his back. Knowing Kong Kui was already under Kuai Kui's control, Duke Chu had to flee with his people to the State of Lu.

Having learned Kong Kui was held under duress, the loyal and honest Zi Lu ran recklessly to rescue his master. On the way Zi Lu ran across Zi Gao, who was also Confucius' disciple and was then an official in Wei. Zi Gao tried to dissuade Zi Lu, saying, "You cannot meddle in politics! Stay away or you are a martyr in vain." Impassioned, Zi Lu exclaimed, "I am fed by the Kong, and I will not leave him alone and run for my life!" Stoutly, Zi Lu dashed to the top of the altar and shouted, "Prince! Why do you detain Kong Kui? Though you kill him, there would still be people standing in your way! You coward! I am setting fire now.

Let's see if you are going to set Kong Kui free when the stage is half burned!" Fuming at such offense, Kuai Kui ordered his fierce warriors to kill Zi Lu. Alone and helpless, Zi Lu soon received a vital stab and fell into blood. Though on his last gasp, Zi Lu managed to sit. He set his hair, put his helmet right, and tied the tassels, saying, "A gentleman does not die with a slanting hat." The crowd was stunned at the sight, watching him putting his helmet and robe right and dying.

Confucius was in the State of Lu when the incident in Wei came into his ears. He naturally thought of his two disciples Zi Gao and Zi Lu who were working there. His heart was laden with anxiety. Confucius could not sleep or eat, and repeatedly talked to himself, "Zi Gao will be back, but Zi Lu is dead!"

There was nobody that understood the disciples better than Confucius himself. He knew each and every of them: Zi Gao would not interfere or meddle in the incident, and would flee back to Lu. Zi Lu, however, had been one that would "challenge a tiger with bare fists and wade a river without a boat with his brute courage", but would always bear in mind the precept of "helping people fearlessly". He knew Zi Lu would not leave Kong Kui alone and run for his own life, therefore the chance for him to survive was bleak. Several days later, what Confucius had anticipated became true when Zi Gao brought back the death of Zi Lu.

Confucius could not help weeping at the death of Zi Lu, and ordered his disciples to hold a memorial ceremony for Zi Lu in the atrium. What broke Confucius' heart even more was the news that Zi Lu was cut into pieces after his death. Having lost his son in his old age, and now losing his favorite disciple, Confucius had a heart that was laden with palpable grief.

Several months later, Confucius fell ill and before long he passed away. Confucius might have realized his days were few when he was anticipating the death of Zi Lu.

49. 诛杀少正卯

孔子担任鲁国大司寇第七天，便杀掉了扰乱朝政的大夫少正卯，并且陈尸三天，作为警示。孔子的这一招令人惊愕，似乎谁都没想到孔子也会开杀戒。他的学生子贡忍不住去拜见，当面询问缘由。

子贡说："少正卯在鲁国是个有名的人，现在您一上台就把他杀掉，会不会是个错误啊？"

孔子反问他："你知道历史上商汤杀了尹谐，文王杀了潘正，周公杀了管叔、蔡叔，太公杀了华士，管仲杀了付乙，子产杀了史何，你说这七个人处在不同的时代，却都一样被杀掉，难道都是错误？"

子贡挠了挠头，"这个……这个……"没说出什么来。

孔子便接着往下说："这七个被杀的人虽然处在不同时代，杀他们的原因却是相同的，他们犯的罪也是相同的。"

子贡听得来神了，"您能说说他们都犯了什么罪？"

孔子让他坐下，慢慢道来："天下有五种重大的罪恶，当然，窃盗不包括在内。这五种分别是：第一，思想叛逆而且凶险；第二，行为邪僻而且固执；第三，言语虚伪而且好辩；第四，总是记那些不义且怪的事，而且搜罗广博；第五，依从不合理的事情还要强释为理。这五种罪，只要具备一种，这个人就会被君子杀掉。你看看这个少正卯，他可以说汇集了这五种罪恶于一身。你没注意到吗？平时他周围总是聚徒成群，他说话的时候足以张扬惑众，他的刚愎自用足以颠倒是非，拉帮结派。这是人群中极为聪明却又奸诈的人，这样的人很容易拉拢一批人，形成群党。你说这能不令人担忧吗？如果不杀他，必定会危及朝政。"

子贡听了，连连点头，也就解了心头疑惑。

孔子不是个书呆子，他有出色的为政才能。他不是只会纸上谈兵，他知道应当仁爱谁，严惩谁。他知道什么时候动嘴，什么时候动手。说仁就是不杀人，恐怕是对孔子的误解。

THE EXECUTION OF SHAO ZHENGMAO

On the seventh day of taking the office of the Minister of Justice, Confucius had his deputy Shao Zhengmao executed for disturbing court governance, and as a warning, had the corpse displayed for three days. It was so stunning and no one had ever expected Confucius could ever resort to a sword. One of his disciples Zi Gong went to him asking for the reason.

Zi Gong asked, "Shao Zhengmao was well known in the State of Lu. Now would it be a real mistake to have him executed when you have just taken your office?"

Confucius asked in reply, "In different times in the long past, Shang Tang killed Yin Xie; King Wen killed Pan Zheng; Duke Zhou killed Guan Shu and Cai Shu; Tai Gong killed Hua Shi; Guan Zhong killed Fu Yi; Zi Chan killed Shi He. Now can you tell me if they were all mistakes?"

Scratching his head, Zi Gong could find no words, "They… they…"

Confucius continued, saying, "They lived in different times, but were killed for the same reasons, and for the same crimes."

Zi Gong became interested, "Then what are their crimes?"

Showing him to the seat, Confucius continued unhurriedly, "Under Heaven there are five serious crimes, not including theft: one, having a recalcitrant mind; two, alienating oneself and refusing changes; three, enjoying specious arguments; four, broadcasting others' faults; and five, supporting and profiting from others' bad deeds. Any one of these five could lead to capital punishment by a gentleman. As to Shao Zhengmao, he had all the five in him. He always had a gang around him. He was masterful of spreading fallacies to deceive people. He had been so self-willed as to distort truth and go for factional setup. He had been extremely smart but deceitful, and inclined to form cliques. Don't you think that is most disturbing? He would sure to be a threat to the court's governance."

Nodding in agreement, Zi Gong had his doubts resolved.

Instead of being a bookworm, Confucius displayed remarkable talents for governance. Instead of being an armchair strategist, he had an eye for those who deserved benevolence and those needed punishment. Confucius understood well the use of his pen and sword as well. It would be mere misinterpretation if one takes his benevolence as a synonym of not killing.

50. 君子不下棋

鲁哀公听别人说君子不下棋，觉得很奇怪，下棋一直是文人的高雅活动啊，怎么又说君子不下棋呢？他就去问孔子。

孔子很肯定地回答鲁哀公确实有这么回事：君子不下棋。哀公不明白，问为什么这么说。孔子答道："因为下棋的时候双方就要互相争胜。"哀公还是不明白，"下棋当然要互相争胜，为什么因为互相争胜就不能下棋呢？"孔子回答说："因为要争胜，就会同时都想着走邪路来获胜。"

哀公感到一阵恐惧。过了一会儿，哀公又接着请教："像这样子的话，可以说明君子对邪路的厌恶是极为强烈的了。"孔子说："是啊，如果君子对邪路的厌恶不强烈，那么对正路的喜爱也不会强烈；如果君子对正路的喜爱不强烈，那么百姓对上位者的爱戴也就不会强烈。《诗》里说：'没有见到那君子，总是忧心忡忡。等我看到他，等我遇到他，我就会满心欢喜。’《诗》里所说的喜好善道也是这么强烈啊！”

哀公感叹地说：“讲得好！君子总是成全别人的好事，而不会促成别人的坏事。要不是您告诉我这些道理，这样的话我是听不到的。”

琴棋书画历来为文人雅士的代表性爱好。没想到孔子对博弈却有微词。争强好胜是喜爱博弈者的特点，谁都不愿意认输，谁都要千方百计地打败对方，所以有兵不厌诈之说。看起来有必要把握智慧、狡诈、邪念、虚伪的真正含义。

A GENTLEMAN DOES NOT PLAY CHESS

Duke Ai of the State of Lu was rather curious when he learned that a gentleman did not play chess. It had been a scholars' sport of high taste, but how could a gentleman not play? Thus he turned to Confucius with the question.

Confucius confirmed on the view: A gentleman would not play chess. Puzzled, Duke Ai asked Confucius the reason.

Confucius answered, "That's because the two sides will vie to win when playing chess."

More puzzled, Duke Ai asked, "When playing chess, we surely would vie to win. But why can't they play chess just because they would vie to win?"

"When vying to win," Confucius said, "One would resort to every means, including evil ones."

Caught in a dread, Duke Ai continued after a pause, "In that case, a gentleman would have intense aversion toward evil means."

"For sure one does," Confucius said. "Should a gentleman hold no intense feeling toward evil means, he would have no intense love for righteous means. Should a gentleman hold no intense love for righteous means, the commoners would have no intense respect for the rulers. In the *Book of Odes*, it's the earnest longing for the righteous means or 'my lord':

While I do not see my lord,
My sorrowful heart is agitated.
Let me have seen him,
Let me have met him,
And my heart will then be stilled."

Hearing that, Duke Ai exclaimed, "Well said! A gentleman always helps others to achieve their moral perfection but not their evil conduct. Were it not from you, I would find nowhere to hear such truth."

Zither, chess, painting and calligraphy had represented the tastes of scholars throughout the history. However, Confucius thought differently on playing chess. Vying for victory had featured gaming as neither side would like to lose — they would try every possible means to defeat the opposite side. Just like the saying goes, nothing is too deceitful in war. It seems there is a need for us to comprehend the true meaning of wisdom, craft, evil, and hypocrisy.

51. 评点子羔为官

子羔担任卫国的监狱官的时候，曾经对一个犯人处以砍脚的刑罚。不久，卫国发生了蒯聩企图从儿子手里夺回王位的政乱，子羔不想卷入这件事，便从卫都出逃。逃到郭门，城门早已经关闭。按命令，士兵不得擅自打开。这时守门的正好是那个被砍了脚的人。他看到子羔慌慌张张地想要逃出城门，就冲着子羔挥挥手，告诉子羔那边城墙有个缺口。可子羔远远地瞅了那缺口一眼，冲守门人摇摇手，“不行，君子不能像盗贼一样翻墙而出！”守门人又告诉子羔另一条路：“那边还有个小洞。”子羔还是摇摇头，说：“不行，君子不能像狗一样从洞里钻出去。”缺了脚的守门人见子羔如此坚决，便告诉他附近有个小房子，那儿比较安全。子羔于是躲进了小房子。

追捕子羔的乱兵没发现子羔，闹哄哄地走了。子羔出来，准备离开。临走，他对守门人说：“当年我为了不损害君主的法律，亲自下令砍去了你的脚。如今我处在危难之中，你正好可以报仇雪恨，可你连着三次指点我逃生之路，为什么呢？”

守门人的回答让子羔听了非常意外，又非常感动：“你下令砍我的脚是我罪该如此，是没有办法改变的事情。在这之前，您依据法律来审理我的案子，先处理了别人，然后才处理我的问题。我知道，这是您在为我争取更多的时间来考虑是否可以免除我的罪过，我心里是很明白的。但是我的罪是确凿的，案件根据事实判决，罪名根据事实确立。到了行刑的时候，您心里是凄凉不悦的，我可以从您的脸色上看出来。我也知道，您跟我并没有私情，您为要砍去我的脚而闷闷不乐，是因为天生的为人之道，君子之道。所以，我其实是对您心悦诚服的，没有怨恨您，也从没想过要报仇。”

后来，孔子知道了这件事，非常肯定子羔的为官与为人。孔子说：“子羔真是善于做官啊！同样是实施法律，心存仁义宽恕就会培植恩德；施加严刑酷法就会招致仇怨。子羔真正能够公正无私地做事。”

孔子对弟子的教育可以说是成功的。他的精神、思想，在弟子身上得到了体现。

APPRAISING ZI GAO'S GOVERNANCE

When he was a warden in the State of Wei, Zi Gao once sentenced a prisoner to be chopped off his feet. Before long, Kuai Kui launched a coup d'état in Wei in an attempt to recapture the throne from his son. Zi Gao wanted to stay clear of the turmoil and fled. When he reached the city gate, it was already shut and the soldier on duty was not allowed to open without an order. It happened that the soldier was the one that had been chopped off his feet. Seeing Zi Gao running in panic, he waved his hand, and showed him a gap on the wall. With a quick look,

Zi Gao shook his head, saying, "No, no! A gentleman does not climb over walls like a thief." The soldier then showed Zi Gao another direction, "Take the hole there!" Shaking his head again, Zi Gao said, "No, no! A gentleman does not crawl through a hole like a dog." Seeing him so resolved, the soldier showed Zi Gao a little hut nearby where he could stay safe. Thus Zi Gao dodged into the hut.

The hunting soldiers could not find Zi Gao and left in a clamor. Zi Gao then wanted to take his leave. Upon parting, he asked the soldier, "When I ordered the penalty on you, I did that to enforce the decrees. Now I am in danger and it's right for your revenge. You have showed me the escape thrice. But why?"

Much surprised and touched, Zi Gao heard the gate keeper say, "When you ordered to have my feet chopped, it was something that you could not alter. You had handled the other cases in accordance to the law before mine. I understood you were making time for me on the chance of pardoning me. I knew that well in my heart. However, my crime was irrefutable and the case was ruled on facts. I knew you felt sad upon my execution. I could tell that from your face. I knew it was wholly out of your personal integrity and moral virtues that you should feel sad, for I had no personal connection with you. Thus I felt convinced. I didn't hate you or think anything of revenge."

Later, Confucius learned that. He approved the governance and conduct of Zi Gao. Confucius remarked, saying, "Zi Gao surely understands governance. While executing laws, if one holds a benevolent and merciful heart, one is to plant the seed of gratitude. If one resorts only to merciless tortures, one is to plant the seed of hatred. Zi Gao could act impartially."

Confucius' education on his disciples can be regarded as a success. His spirit and thoughts found their full play in his disciples.

52. 怎么学柳下惠

鲁国柳下惠坐怀不乱的故事广为流传。说是那夜因为郭门已经关了，柳下惠只得露宿在郭门。恰好有个女子也来，她也出不去，只好等天亮。夜晚很冷，也没有什么被褥可以御寒，柳下惠担心女子被冻死，就让她坐在自己怀里。这样直到天亮，柳下惠没有对女子产生什么邪念。

后来还是鲁国，有个男子独自一人住在一间屋里，邻居是个寡妇，也是独自住一屋。有天夜里，狂风大雨，撕坏了寡妇的房子。寡妇没有办法，到邻居男子那儿敲门，恳请寄宿。男子关住门就是不开，不让寡妇进去。寡妇在门外大声问他："你为什么这么不讲仁义，明知道我在屋外淋雨受冻，却不让我进屋呢？"男子很礼貌地回答说："我听说男女不到六十岁是不能同居一室的。眼下你年轻，我也年轻，因此不敢让你进来。"

寡妇抱着希望问："你为什么不能像柳下惠那样，在怀里抱了那个没来得及出郭门的女人整整一夜，也没有人说他淫乱啊。"男子老老实实地回答："柳下惠可以做到，我知道自己做不到。我只能用我自己的方式来学习柳下惠了。"

这件事传到了孔子耳里。孔子赞叹说："真是不错。想学柳下惠的人很多，还没有人用过类似的方式。追求一种最好的境界，却不死板地袭用某一种具体的做法，这真的是明智啊！"

这个男子用这种看似冷酷的方法解决了这个微妙而且可怕的问题，赢得的是体面和安宁。那个被淋的女子日后也一定庆幸自己只是被雨淋了，而不是被淹没在众人的唾沫中。其实人的能力有大有小，境界的修炼有许多不同的途径，只要目标达到了，即使在常人看来是笨拙的方法又有什么不可以呢？

HOW TO LEARN FROM LIUXIA HUI?

The story of Liuxia Hui in the State of Lu had been popular. It was late in the day, and the city gates were already closed when Liuxia Hui got there. Thus he had to put up in the gate for the night. It so happened that a young lady also got there late and had to stay overnight. As night neared, it became very cold and nothing was available to keep warm. Liuxia Hui was afraid that the lady would get frozen. He had her sit on his lap until the next morning, himself remaining free of any evil thought.

Later on it happened again in the State of Lu that a man lived alone in a hut. His next-door neighbor was a widow and lived alone too. In a stormy night the widow's hut was torn broken. Helpless as she was, the widow ran to the man's door requesting lodging. The man, however, would not let her in. The widow lady cried outside his door, "How come you are so ruthless? You know I'm in such a cold storm, but would not let me in!" With the best of his proprieties, the man said, "I have heard that strange man and woman under age 60 should not stay in one room. You are young and I'm young, too. Thus I dare not let you in."

Still holding some hope, the widow asked, "Can't you behave like Liuxia Hui? He kept a lady on his lap for a night in the city gate, and nobody has said anything bad of him." Earnestly, the man said, "Liuxia Hui could do that, but I know I could not. Thus I have to learn from him in my way."

Confucius heard of the story, and admired, "That's good! There have been many that want to learn from Liuxia Hui, but nobody except him had thought of such a way. It is wise to pursue an ideal but not stick to stereotypes."

The man won himself grace and peace on the delicate but horrible problem in a way though much too cold hearted. The lady should have rejoiced in her being drenched in the storm instead of gossips. In fact, the level of attainment one could reach depends on his talents. If only the goal is reached, it might work as well for however clumsy a means in other's mind.

53. 荐贤能者为真贤

子贡问孔子说：“如今做臣子的，谁可以称得上是贤者啊？”孔子摇了摇头，“我不知道。要说从前吧，齐国的鲍叔、郑国的子皮，他俩应该就是贤者。”

子贡很诧异，“齐国不是还有管仲，郑国不是还有子产吗？难道他俩不是贤者？”孔子还是摇摇头，“端木赐啊，你真是只知道一，不知道二啊。你说说看，是一个使出自己气力的人贤良呢还是一个举荐贤能的人贤良呢？”子贡毫不思索地脱口而出：“当然是举荐贤能的人更贤良啊！”孔子微微一笑，“那不就对了吗？我听说鲍叔牙推荐了管仲，子皮推荐了子产。而从没有听说管仲和子产二人推荐过比自己更有贤能的人士。”

秦国的伯乐，因为善于发现千里马，而获得很高的称赞。后人因此说“千里马常有而伯乐不常有”。孔子推鲍叔、子皮而剔管仲、子产，合情合理。

HE WHO RECOMMENDS THE VIRTUOUS IS THE TRULY VIRTUOUS

Zi Gong asked Confucius, "Among all those ministers, who would you say are the virtuous?"

Shaking his head, Confucius said, "I have no idea. If we say those of the former times, I would name Bao Shuya in the State of Qi and Zi Pi in the State of Zheng."

Puzzled, Zi Gong said, "Then what about Guan Zhong in Qi and Zi Chan in Zheng? Aren't they the virtuous?"

Shaking his head, Confucius said, "Zi Gong, you are aware of only one aspect and ignorant of the other. Tell me now, between one who exerts his own efforts and one who recommends a virtuous, who is more virtuous?"

"For sure, it's the one who recommends!" Zi Gong said without hesitation.

Smiling, Confucius said, "There you go! I have heard that Bao Shuya recommended Guan Zhong, and Zi Pi recommended Zi Chan, but never heard of any significant recommendations by Guan Zhong and Zi Chan."

Bo Le in the State of Qin had acquired a big fame for his judgment of *Qianlima*, thoroughbred horses with stamina. There has been the saying "For winged steeds they are common, but a Bo Le is rare." Therefore, it stands to good reason that Confucius put Bao Shuya and Zi Pi ahead of Guan Zhong and Zi Chan.

54. 宓子贱的成功之道

宓子贱跟从孔子学习，后来担任单父这个地方的长官，做得很不错，深受当地民众的喜爱。孔子得知后，便采访了宓子贱。

“你治理单父，那里的人民都很高兴。你是采取了什么措施而得到他们的拥护的呢？”孔子问。“我当人民的父母官，就像当父亲的爱抚他的儿子一样；我也像他们的儿子一样爱抚所有的孤儿，并为他们的丧事表示哀痛。”宓子贱答道。“好。不过这些都还是小的善行，可以使百姓亲近你，但还不足以受拥护。”孔子进了一步。“我把三个人当作父亲来看待；把五个人当作兄长来看待，把十一个人当作朋友来看待。”宓子贱回答了孔子。“把三个人当作父亲来对待，可以用来教育人们恪守孝道；把五个人当作兄长来对待，可以用来教育人们敬爱兄长；把十一个人当作朋友来对待，可以用来作为举荐德才兼备的人的榜样。不过，这些也只能算是中等的善行，可以使普通人来亲近你，但还不足以受拥护。”孔子还是不满意宓子贱的回答。“我找到了当地五个比我贤明的人，我侍奉他们，并从他们那儿接受指点，他们教给我很多的为政方法。”宓子贱想了想又补充说。

听到这儿，孔子长嘘了一口气说道：“这才是成就大业的关键所在啊！从前尧舜治理天下，也是致力于搜求贤人来辅佐自己。贤人是民众得到福佑的根本，可惜啊，宓子贱治理的这个地方太小了。”

孔子从弟子的政绩中、从弟子的口中得到了双重的证明，贤能的人、举荐贤能的人、尊崇贤能的人，是百姓的福音。

THE KEY TO SUCCESS FOR MI ZIJIAN

Mi Zijian studied after Confucius. Later he served as the chief minister in Shanfu. His governance gained him quite a good reputation, and he was therefore quite popular among the people. Having learned that, Confucius had a talk with him.

"Under your governance, people in Shanfu lived happy lives." Confucius asked, "What measures have you adopted to get their support?"

"Being their parental official, I cared for them as a father to his son." Mi Zijian told him, "I looked after the orphans as a son to a father. I shared their sorrows for their dead parents."

"Well done!" Confucius continued, "But these are just trifles that drew you close to your people, but not to the extent of endorsement."

Mi Zijian explained to Confucius, saying, "When there are three men, I regard them as my fathers. When there are five men, I regard them as my elder brothers. When there are eleven men, I regard them as my friends."

Not quite satisfied, Confucius went on, saying, "When you regard the three men as your fathers, you teach them filial piety. When you regard the five men as your elder brothers, you teach them respect for seniors. When you regard the eleven men as your friends, you set an example for recommending people with talents and virtues. However, these are merely measures of medium benevolence that could draw average ones close to you, but not yet to the extent of endorsement."

Pondering for a moment, Mi Zijian added, "I found five men that were wiser than me. I served them, and received their instructions. They taught me quite a few tips on governance."

At that Confucius sighed in comfort, saying, "That is the key to achieving a grand cause. In ancient times when Yao and Shun were governing their lands under Heaven, they were committed to finding wise men for their assistance. The wise men are the bliss for the people. But, if only the place you govern were not so small a land!"

From the achievements and talks of his disciples, Confucius double-checked the truth that the real bliss for the people should be those talents who could recommend and revere talents.

55. 为官的得失

孔子的跛脚哥哥有个儿子叫孔篾，跟宓子贱在一块儿做官。孔子路过孔篾那儿，就跟他聊了聊，问问他的工作生活情况：“你做官也有一段时间了，你觉得你得到了什么？有没有失去什么？”孔篾的回答让孔子出乎意料。“我没得到什么，却失去了三个方面。政事一件接一件，没完没了，所学的知识都没有时间温习，这样学习就不能真正明了；工资么又太低，连碗稀饭都无法供给亲戚，因而骨肉亲情在日益疏远；又因为公事烦多并且紧急，腾不出时间去吊唁死者探望病人，所以对朋友也做得很不够。就是这三个方面，我觉得失去的。”孔子听了很不高兴。

后来，孔子又路过宓子贱那儿，也跟他聊了聊，问题还是一样的“你当了官，你觉得你得到了什么？有没有失去什么？”宓子贱的回答也让孔子出乎意料。“我做了官以后，我没有失去什么，却在三个方面有不少收获。第一，当初您教导的那些道理，现在得到了实践，这样学习就更明了了；第二，工资虽然不高，但足够维持生活，还可以有些盈余来照顾亲戚，这样骨肉亲情就更加密切了；第三，尽管平时总是忙于公务，可只要挤挤时间，总还可以兼顾吊唁死者或者探望病人，这样朋友之间的关系也就更加紧密了。”

孔子听到孔篾与宓子贱截然不同的两种回答，十分感叹，连连称赞宓子贱是个君子。

当官会带来什么，不同的人有不同的结果。为什么都是当官，结果却大不相同，这至少与为官之道有关系。可以说，宓子贱与孔篾是道不同，道不同感受就不一样了。其实世界上没有什么绝对的东西，要不然社会就不会有什么官迷和隐士、贪官与清官了。

THE GAINS AND LOSSES OF BEING AN OFFICIAL

Confucius' crippled brother had a son named Kong Mie working in the same area with Mi Zijian. Confucius once passed by Kong Mie and had a chat with him, asking about his life and work, saying, "You have taken the office for quite a while. What do you think you have gained and lost?"

"I have gained nothing," his reply was quite beyond what Confucius had expected, "but have lost three. The endless work has cost all my time. For what I have learned I could find no time to review, thus I was unable to explore the true meanings. The pay is so low that hardly could I offer even a bowl of porridge to my relatives. My family relationship has become estranged. My full and busy agenda even cost my time to visit the ill, making me rather indebted to my friends. These are the three I have lost." Hearing all that, Confucius was rather upset.

Later on while passing by Mi Zijian, Confucius went for a chat too and asked him the same question, "You have taken the office for quite a while. What do you think you have gained or lost?"

"Ever since I took the position, I have lost nothing but gained three," his reply was quite beyond what Confucius had expected too. "Firstly, I have put to practice what you have instructed, and now I have gained a better understanding on how to study. Secondly, despite the low pay, I got just enough to sustain my life, and even some extra to help my relatives. That way my family relationship has got strengthened. Thirdly, despite the busy work, I could still find some time to pay respect to the dead or visit the ill. That way my friendship has got closer."

Confucius was filled with mixed hearts for the contrastive responses of Kong Mie and Mi Zijian. He hailed Mi Zijian as a real gentleman.

For different people, there would be different gains while in an official career. All are officials, but why different? That has a lot to do with the Way of being an official as exemplified by Mi Zijian and Kong Mie. Nothing goes absolute in this world, or there should be no such people like career addicts and hermits, corrupt and honest officials.

